Chapter 1 How Geography is assessed

Introduction: What is assessed in each paper?

Figure 1.1 shows what is assessed on each of the three exam papers. There are no options within the papers – you must answer **all** the questions. The final exam paper tests your ability to 'think like a geographer' and provides you with a geographical issue. You must explore and reach decisions about how the issue should be managed.

Figure 1.1 What each exam paper assesses

What is assessed in the paper?	How is it assessed?
Paper 1: Our Natural World (physical geography) Topics assessed: ■ Global hazards ■ Changing climate ■ Distinctive landscapes ■ Sustaining ecosystems ■ Physical fieldwork	**Time allowed:** 1 hour 30 minutes **Marks:** 70 **Percentage of final grade:** 35% The highest number of marks are for 6- and 8-mark questions, which are mostly related to case studies.
Paper 2: People and Society (human geography) Topics assessed: ■ Urban futures ■ Dynamic development ■ UK in the 21st century ■ Resource reliance ■ Human fieldwork	**Time allowed:** 1 hour 30 minutes **Marks:** 70 **Percentage of final grade:** 35% The highest number of marks are for 6- and 8-mark questions, which are mostly related to case studies.
Paper 3: Geographical Exploration ■ Geographical skills ■ Decision-making exercise	**Time allowed:** 1 hour 30 minutes **Marks:** 60 **Percentage of final grade:** 30% The allocated time includes the time to read the Resource Booklet. This paper contains smaller skills-based questions as well as two extended 12-mark questions.

How to use this workbook

This workbook contains a chapter for each of the three exam papers you will complete as part of your GCSE course. In each chapter, you will practise the full range of question styles.

Apart from revising the content of the course, examiners are specifically highlighting three important areas for students to focus their attention on in preparation for the exam:

1. Being able to use geographical skills, including knowledge of different maps and graphs and how to interpret them.
2. Being able to use numerical skills, including ratios, mean and percentages.
3. Being able to apply case study knowledge and understanding to questions that require you to evaluate or assess, and to reach conclusions.

Write your answers in the spaces provided and use your own notebook if you run out of space.

Understanding the exam questions

This chapter is about how Paper 1 and Paper 2 of your GCSE Geography are assessed. It will explore:
- what the command word in the question is telling you to do in your answer
- how to tackle questions that use skills relating to graphs, maps and statistics
- how to answer questions worth 6 and 8 marks, where you are required to be evaluative.

Paper 1 and Paper 2 contain a wide variety of question styles, ranging from 1 mark to 8 marks. The final question has an additional 3 marks for spelling, punctuation and grammar. It is important that you understand what each question is asking you to do.

- **Command words** are mostly at the beginning of the question and they tell you HOW to write your response. You will need to write a very different answer for a 'define' question compared with an 'evaluate' question.
- The **marks** that are available for each question are always highlighted at the end of the space where you write your answer. You need to write an answer of an appropriate length. Do not spend too long on a 2-mark question. The space provided gives you an idea of how much you should write.
- The **assessment objective (AO)** is what the examiner is looking for in your response. There are four AOs (see Figure 1.2). Some questions assess AO1 and AO4 only and have a low number of marks available. Other, longer questions assess a combination of different AOs and will require you to show more of your understanding combined with an ability to reach judgements.

> Although the space provided does indeed help you to know how much to write, do not be limited by this. There is space at the back of the exam paper and on additional sheets for you to continue an answer. This is particularly relevant to the 6- and 8-mark questions where you might need to write more. Make sure you write the question number clearly in the margin of any additional space you use.

Figure 1.2 The assessment objectives (AOs)

	Objective description	Possible command words
AO1	**Knowledge** (facts) about locations, places, processes, environments and different scales.	Describe, Define, Outline, State
AO2	**Understanding** of concepts and how places and processes are linked	Explain how, Explain reasons, Discuss
AO3	Making **judgements** by interpreting and analysing geographical knowledge and understanding from AO1 and AO2	Assess, Evaluate, Suggest, To what extent
AO4	**Geographical skills and techniques** – selecting, using and adapting skills and communicating your findings	Describe the pattern, Calculate, Identify, Give, Suggest

BUG the question

The first challenge in the exam is trying to work out what the question is asking you to do. This is guided by the command word. If you are asked to 'define' then you know that you need to write what a geographical word means; if you are asked to 'assess' then you know you must reach a judgement by the end of your answer.

To avoid writing everything you think you know about the topic in the question, take some time in the exam to process the question. Make sure you do not start writing until you know HOW you are writing your answer and WHAT you are writing about. To do this, **BUG** the question (see Figure 1.3).

B	Put a **box** around the command word that tells you how to write your answer.
U	**Underline** any geographical key words and/or words that are important to the answer, e.g. factors or reasons.
G	**Glance** over the question again. Have you understood what it is asking you to do? Can you rephrase it more simply? Keep glancing back at the question while you write your answer to make sure you are still answering it.

① Explain why the soil in the tropical rainforest does not contain many nutrients. **3 marks**

- Give reasons for how and why
- Not the litter or biomass store
- The question is about the nutrient cycle
- This tells you which biome to focus on

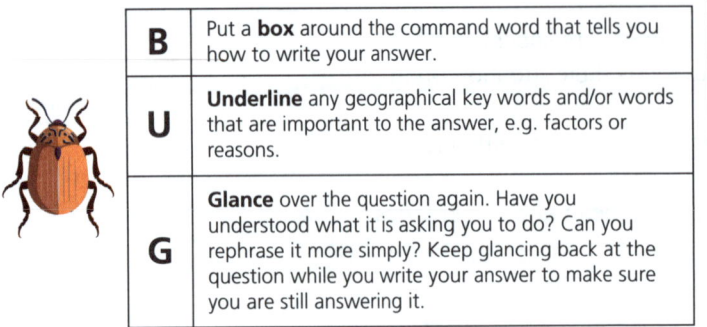

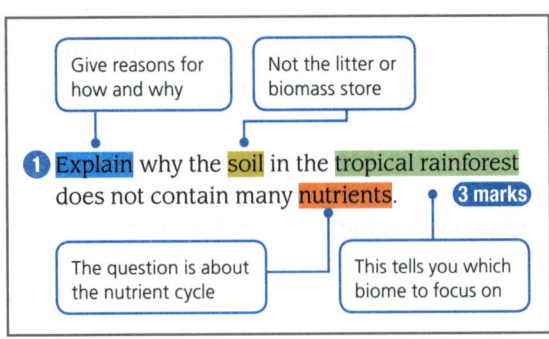

Figure 1.3 BUG the question

4

Dealing with complex questions

Some questions are quite long and contain different elements, all of which need to be tackled in your answer. Break the question down into bits to understand what the examiner wants you to do. Look out for:

- **the command word:** this is often, but not always, the first word in the question
- **instructions to use a figure:** this will be a photo, graph, map or some text in the exam paper. You must refer to the evidence in the source if you have been told to do so.
- **instructions to use a case study or example:** there are ten main case studies and some smaller examples that you could be asked about. When a case study is required, it will usually say '**CASE STUDY**'. If you are not directly asked to write about your case study, it still might be useful to include case study examples.
- **whether you need to write about more than one thing:** for example, the social and environmental impacts of climate change. You need to write about both aspects equally to get a good mark overall.

You are NOT being asked to write about your AC example. You will need specific facts and details about the LIDC or EDC city case study

Give reasons for how and why

You are being asked to write about migrants coming from other countries (not *within* the country)

1. For an LIDC or EDC city that you have studied, explain how international migration has changed the character of the city.

   6 marks

The nature and way of life in the city

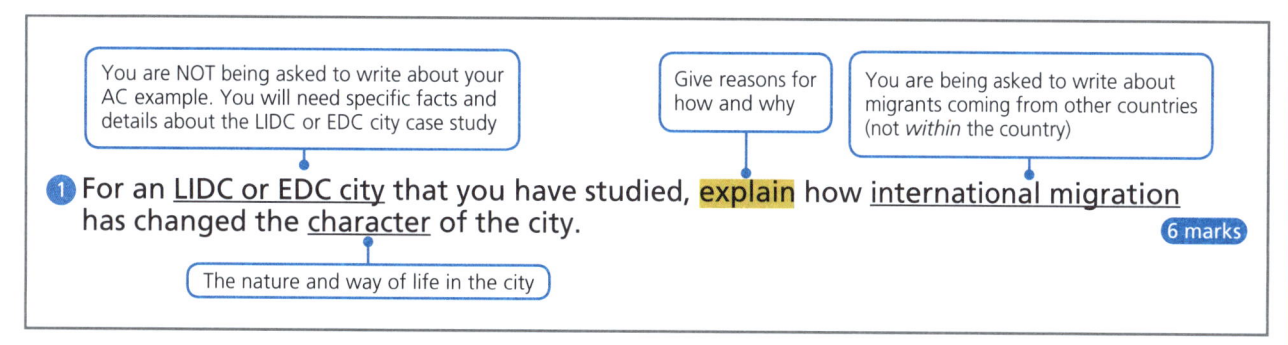

Figure 1.4 Using BUG to understand a 6-mark question

The power of the command word

Figure 1.5 shows you how questions on one possible topic – Ageing populations from the UK in the 21st century – can be assessed through a variety of command words.

Figure 1.5 Command words

Command word	What you need to do	Example of a question	Mark
Calculate	Work out… Marks are sometimes available for the process (workings) and the correct answer.	Calculate the mean of the ages of residents in Sidmouth.	1
State	Briefly write the main point.	State one reason why the UK's population is ageing.	1
Describe	Give an account of something.	Describe a cause of the UK's ageing population.	2
Explain	Give reasons for how and why something happens.	Explain why the UK's population is ageing.	4
Assess	Weigh up whether a statement is true. Evaluate a situation.	Assess the causes of an ageing population in the UK.	6
Evaluate	Give your verdict after providing evidence which both agrees with and contradicts an argument, e.g. positives/negatives of an ageing population.	Evaluate the consequences of an ageing population on the economy of the UK.	8

Skills questions

For your GCSE Geography qualification, 25 per cent of the marks available is based on your ability to select, adapt and use geographical skills and communicate your findings clearly. Exam questions testing these skills will include command words such as 'calculate', 'identify' and 'make a prediction'. You might also be asked to choose an appropriate method of data presentation or to suggest how a method could be improved.

Geographical skills questions appear throughout all three exam papers so it is really important that you understand how to approach them. There are three main skills that you will be tested on:
- using and interpreting maps
- using and interpreting graphs
- numerical and statistical skills.

Using and interpreting maps

You will see a wide variety of maps used within all exam papers, ranging from choropleth maps to flow line maps. You will also have some **AO4 skills questions** which will ask you to do something in relation to these maps, such as measuring distance and reading height measurements.

Different types of maps

Figure 1.6 contains some of the more unusual maps so that you can easily spot them in the exam. You might get a multiple choice exam question which asks you to identify the type of map used in one of the figures within the Resource Booklet.

> Look carefully at the wording of questions asking you to interpret a map or graph. If the question contains the phrase 'using data', it will be worth 4 marks, but if it does not then it will be worth 3 marks. The extra mark is for the use of specific data/numbers.

Figure 1.6 Types of maps

Map type		Description
Choropleth maps	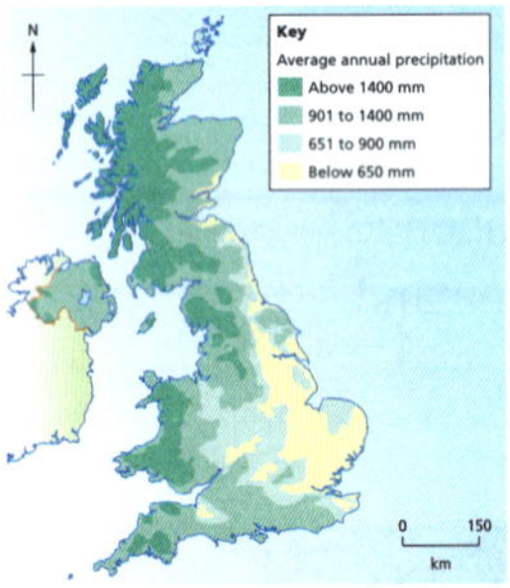	**Choropleth maps** use shading, colour or symbols inside defined areas to show the average values or the quantity of something within those areas.
Isoline maps	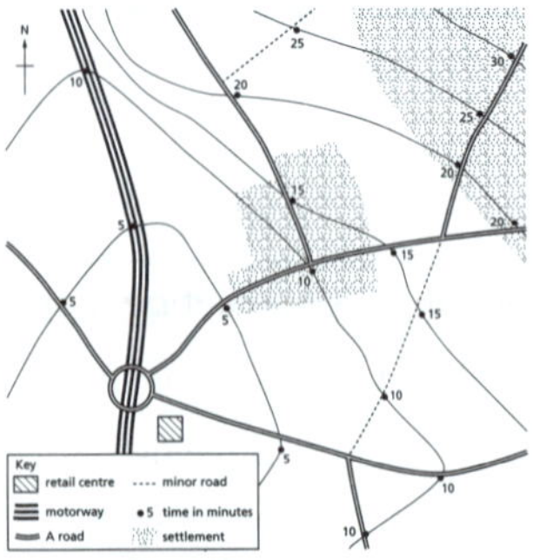	**Isoline maps** have lines which join places that share a common value. We often see these on weather maps as isobars and on OS maps as colour lines or isoheights. The prefix 'iso' means equal.
Flow line maps	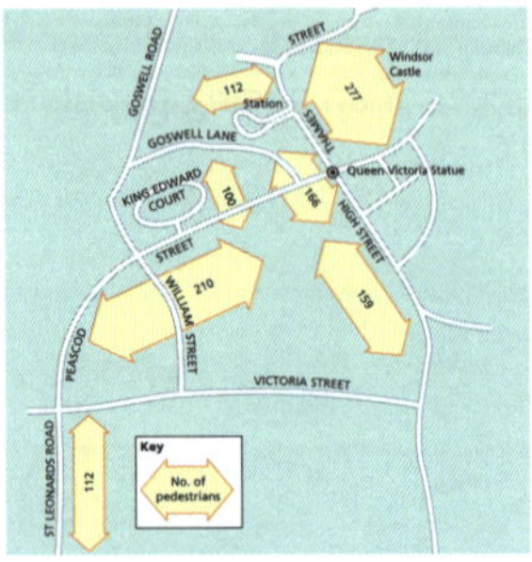	**Flow line maps** are used to show movement or flows such as the flow of migrants or commuters. The line joins the origin to the destination. The direction of the flow is usually indicated by an arrow at the destination end. The lines are usually of different widths to indicate the volume of the flow. **Desire line maps** are similar, but they show destination only and do not change in width.

Sphere of influence maps		**Sphere of influence maps** show how far a feature or place influences people, such as how far people would travel to get to a new shopping mall. Each section might indicate 15-minute journey times.
Thematic maps		**Thematic maps** show a particular theme or topic for a geographical area. This could be average rainfall, geology or the average income of an area. They do not feature any other information such as rivers, cities or highways, only the theme the map is designed to show.

Describing patterns

Figure 1.7 shows the distribution of tropical storms around the world.

Figure 1.7 The global distribution of tropical storms

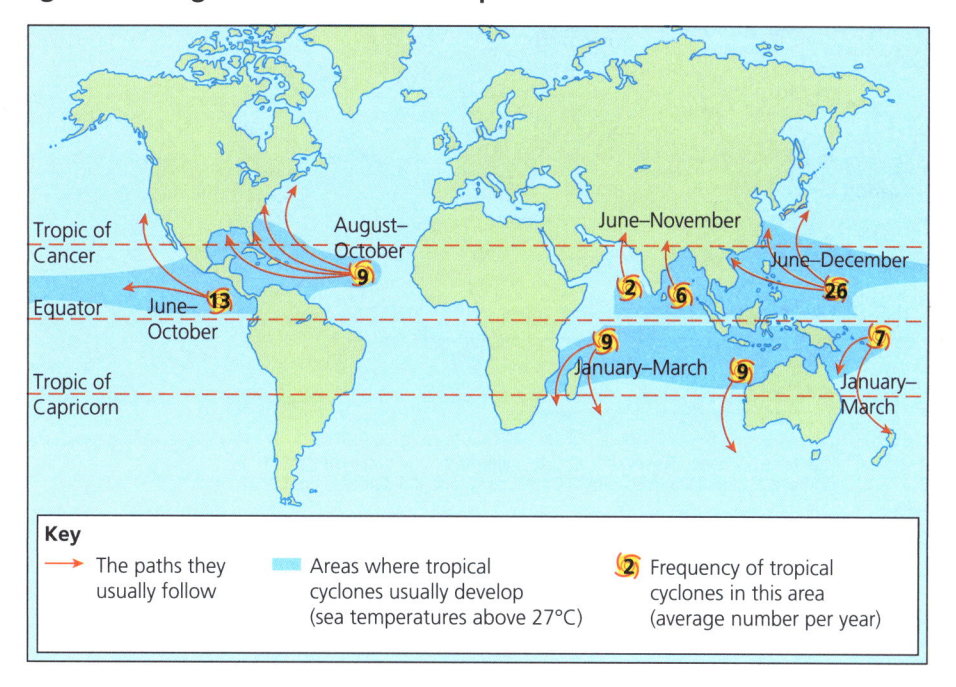

> Describe = say what you see.
>
> Explain = give reasons for what you see. Do not give reasons in a 'describe' question.

① Describe the global distribution of tropical storms.   **3 marks**

Student response

Tropical storms are mostly found between 5° and 15° north and south of the Equator. They are found along the southern states of the USA, in the Caribbean, and in areas of South East Asia such as the Philippines. They can also be found in the Indian Ocean.

> This answer has an opening sentence that describes the general trend; the overall pattern in the distribution. The answer then continues to provide more specific examples of places in the world. Note that this question is worth 3 marks because there is no mention of using data.

> When describing patterns and locations on a global scale, it is often useful to think about **CLOCC**. This stands for:
>
> **C**ompass directions
> **L**ines of latitude/longitude
> **O**ceans and seas
> **C**ontinents
> **C**ountries

7

The following question requires the use of data.

> **2** Using data from Figure 1.8, describe the pattern of the population density in London. **4 marks**

Figure 1.8 The population density of London, 2010

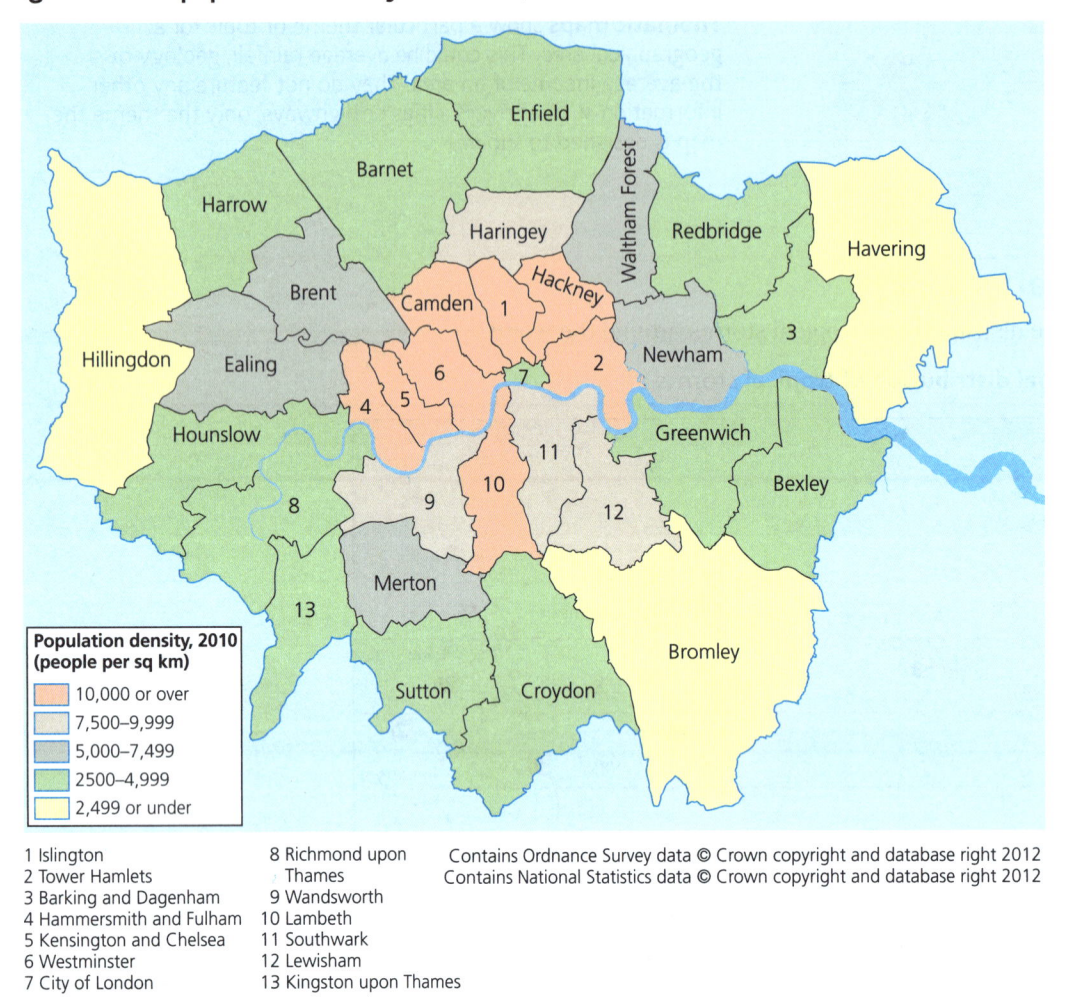

Population density, 2010 (people per sq km)
- 10,000 or over
- 7,500–9,999
- 5,000–7,499
- 2500–4,999
- 2,499 or under

1 Islington
2 Tower Hamlets
3 Barking and Dagenham
4 Hammersmith and Fulham
5 Kensington and Chelsea
6 Westminster
7 City of London
8 Richmond upon Thames
9 Wandsworth
10 Lambeth
11 Southwark
12 Lewisham
13 Kingston upon Thames

Contains Ordnance Survey data © Crown copyright and database right 2012
Contains National Statistics data © Crown copyright and database right 2012

> **3** Below is a student answer, but with missing words and numbers. Complete the gaps, using the key to help you.

Student answer

The highest population densities are towards the .... of London. Most of the highest population densities are .... of the River Thames in areas such as .... and Tower Hamlets with a population of .... , with the exception of .... which is south of the River Thames. Areas like Brent and Ealing in the .... of London have a population density of .... The lowest population densities of .... are in areas such as .... and Havering.

> **4** Read the answer again. Highlight the three parts of the GCSE structure (see below) in different colours.

The answer on the left uses the **GCSE structure**.

General Comment – think about the whole map. What is the general trend you notice?

Specific data – the use of numbers from the key shows that you can read the source.

Exceptions – is there anything that doesn't fit the pattern?

How to read an OS map

Four-figure grid references: To work out the four-figure reference for the star in Figure 1.9, you need to read 'along the corridor' before reading 'up the stairs'. Put an L in the bottom left-hand corner of the box as this helps you to know which lines you need to read. The answer is 6133.

Six-figure grid references: This time you need to know how far into the box a particular landmark is. You need to imagine that the big box has been divided into 10 vertical lines and 10 horizontal lines. It is useful to work out the four-figure grid reference first (62 _ 33 _). Let's work out 'how far' into the 62 box you need to go before reaching the shaded box and 'how far' into the 33 box as well. Our six-figure grid reference becomes 626334.

Figure 1.9 Reading an OS map

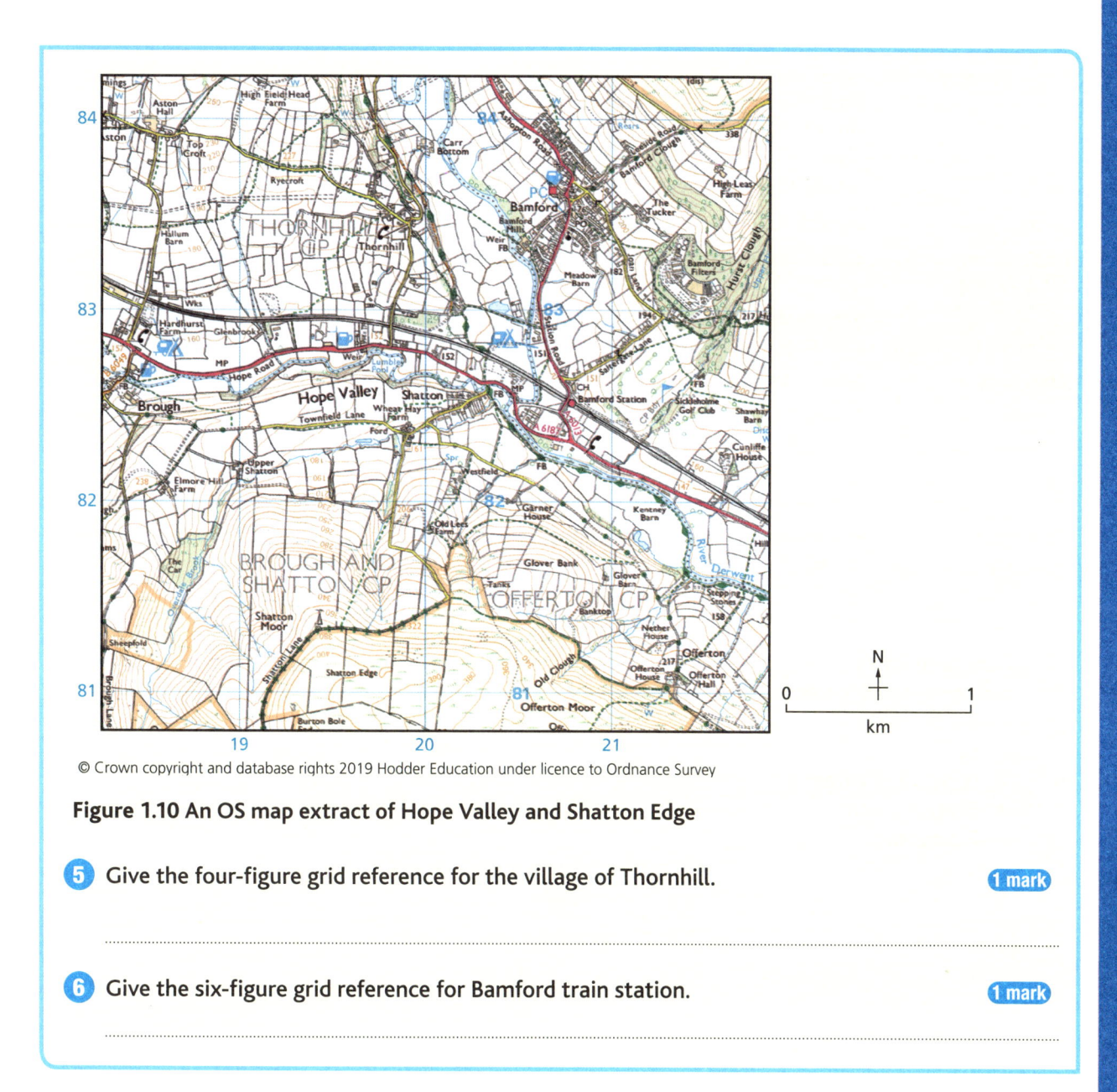

Figure 1.10 An OS map extract of Hope Valley and Shatton Edge

5 Give the four-figure grid reference for the village of Thornhill. *1 mark*

6 Give the six-figure grid reference for Bamford train station. *1 mark*

Using and interpreting graphs

There are many possible types of graph that you might have to use and interpret in your exam. Sometimes you might be asked to suggest the best way to present some data or to demonstrate that you can read the graph, and other times you might be asked a more detailed question requiring you to describe the trend/pattern on the graph.

Types of graph

Figure 1.11 The types of graph you can expect to find in your exam

Graph type	Description
Bar graph	Rectangular bars to show how values vary. They can be vertical, horizontal or divided (which shows them all on one bar).
Histogram	Used to show continuous data (e.g. time, number of miles) instead of discrete variables. The horizontal axis is a scale rather than labels.
Line graph	Plotted as a series of points and then connected with straight lines.
	Used to compare two sets of data. A line of best fit goes roughly through the middle of the points on the graph.
Dispersion graph	Points are plotted against an individual line on a vertical scale. Multiple lines can be drawn on the same graph. They are great for showing the range of the data and how plots are distributed within the range.
	Different size sectors of a circle represent data, like slices of a pie. The larger the slice, the greater the value it represents.
Climate graph	A combination of a bar graph (to show rainfall) and a line graph (to show temperature).
Proportional symbols map	Circles are used to represent the data, with the size of the circle being used to represent the quantity of the variable.
	Representing data using pictures, e.g. for a traffic survey the results could be shown as a picture of a car, bike and bus representing how many were counted.
Cross-section	Shows the shape of the landscape, giving a side view of the shape of the land.
	Shows the distribution of various age groups in a population. It can be created for an area, a whole continent or country, or an individual town, city or village.
	Shows multiple variables on the same graph, but they must all have the same scale (e.g. 0–10). Points can then be connected with lines.
Rose chart	Has equal-sized segments extending from a centre which are proportional to the value they represent.

> **7** Complete Figure 1.11 by writing the missing types of graph next to the correct definitions:
> - Pie chart
> - Radial graph
> - Population pyramid
> - Scatter graph
> - Pictogram

10

8 What type of graph is shown in Figure 1.12?

....

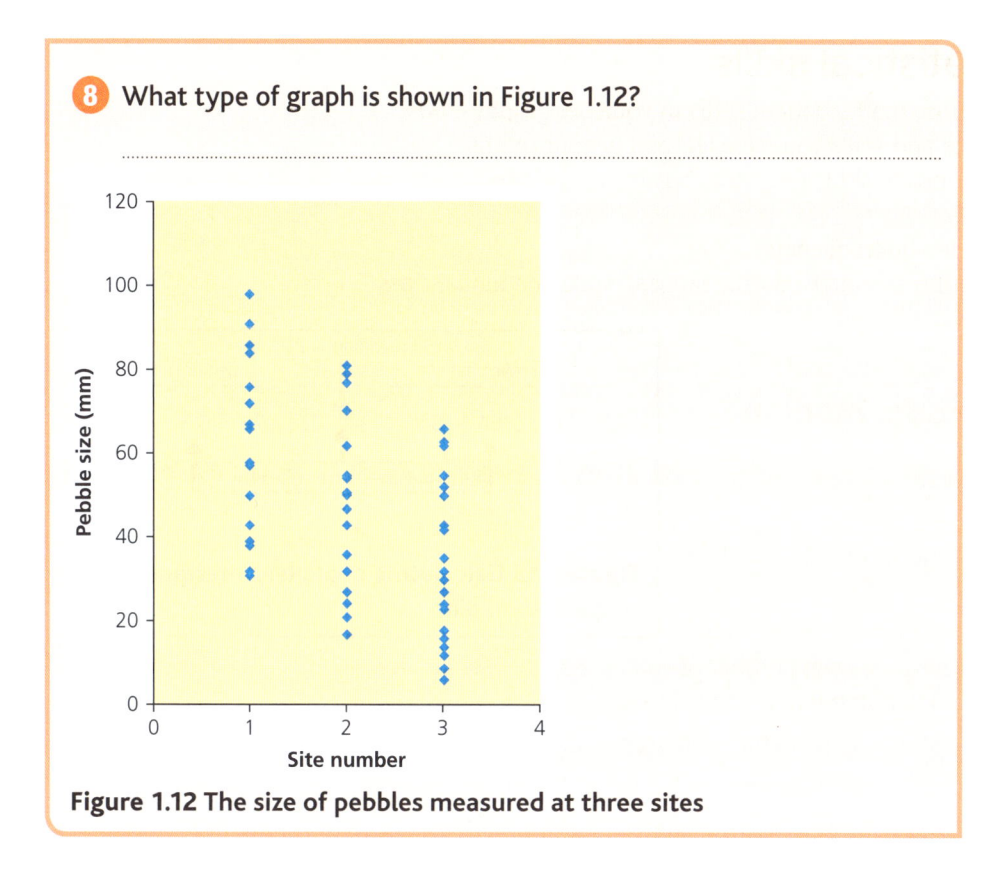

Figure 1.12 The size of pebbles measured at three sites

Describing patterns on graphs

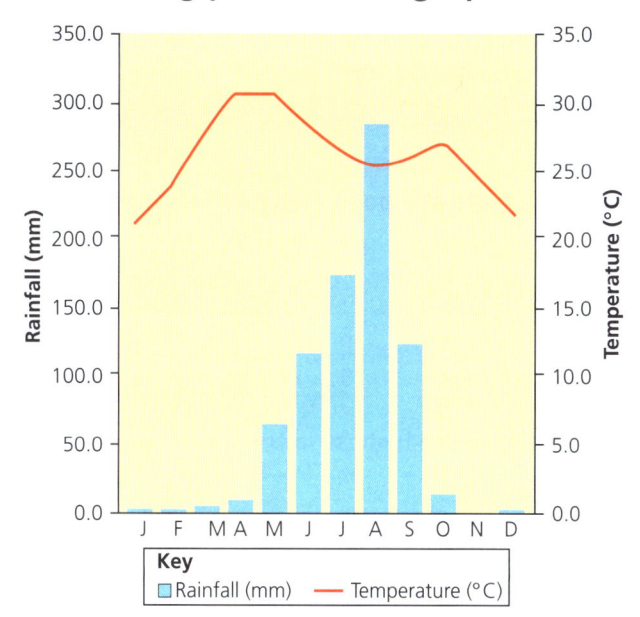

Figure 1.13 Climate graph for Kano, Nigeria

9 Using data, describe the annual pattern of rainfall in Kano, Nigeria (see Figure 1.13). **4 marks**

Student answer

The majority of the rainfall is between May and September and lowest between October and April. The highest rainfall is 275mm in August and the lowest is 0.1mm in December, January and February. Rainfall occurs every month, with the exception of November when there is little to no rainfall recorded.

An alternative exam technique to **GCSE** (shown on page 8) is to use **TEA**, which stands for:

Trend

Example

Anomaly.

Either acronym will remind you to do the same thing, but you might find TEA more memorable.

One mark is given for communicating your answer in a logical order. Using a technique such as TEA helps to give your answer a clear structure.

Chapter 1 How Geography is assessed

11

Numerical and statistical skills

You will also be assessed on your mathematical skills in your Geography exam. These are the same techniques and skills you have learned in your maths lessons. Some of the most important skills for you to be able to use are:
- area and scale
- proportion, ratio, magnitude and frequency
- median, mean, range, quartiles and inter-quartile ranges, mode and modal class
- percentages
- drawing lines of best fit.

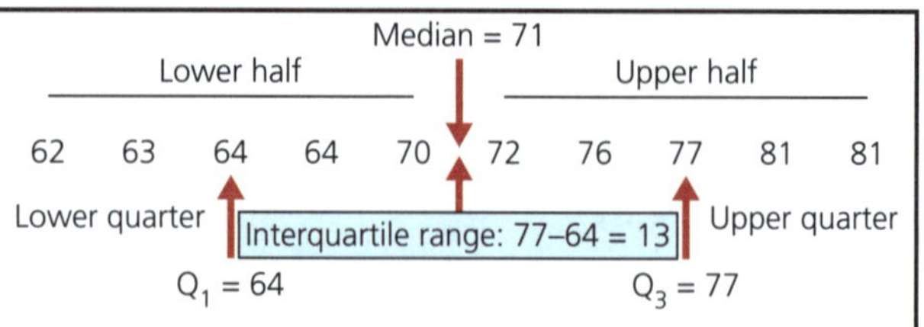

Calculating mean, mode, median and quartile ranges

Look at Figure 1.15.

Mean: add up all the values in the set of data and then divide by the number of values.

Median: arrange the data in rank order. The median is the value in the middle. If you have an even number of values in your data set, for example 10, add the fifth and sixth number and divide by two.

Mode: the value in your data set that appears the most frequently.

Modal class: if there are categories to the data set (e.g. 1–5 cm, 6–10 cm, 11–15 cm), then the modal class is the category that has the highest frequency of results.

Range: the difference between the highest and the lowest values.

Lower quartile: the middle of the lower half of a data set.

Upper quartile: the middle of the upper half of a data set.

Interquartile range: the difference between the values that are one-quarter and three-quarters through a set of data.

Figure 1.15 Calculating quartiles, interquartile range and median

Study Figure 1.16, which shows a set of data collected by students at a point along a river. They have measured the width of the sediment in centimetres.

Figure 1.16 Data for the width of sediment along a river

Sample no	1	2	3	4	5	6	7	8	9	10
Width (cm)	16	3	9	20	12	8	4	8	18	17

10 In the space provided below, write the data set in order from the highest to the lowest number so that you can easily see the range of results.

11 Calculate the following statistics for the data set in Figure 1.16. You might find it useful to annotate the data set in a similar way to that modelled in Figure 1.15.

Mean	
Median	
Mode	
Range	
Lower quartile	
Upper quartile	
Interquartile range	

Calculating percentages

You may also be asked to calculate percentages. A percentage is a way of expressing part of a whole. Look at Figure 1.17. There are 46 megacities in the world. The whole number in this case is 46 and this represents 100 per cent. If 23 of these cities were all in the same continent, that would be 50 per cent of the whole. To calculate the percentage of megacities that are in China, follow these steps using the data in Figure 1.17.

Step 1: Divide the number of megacities in China (15) by the total number of megacities (46).

Step 2: Multiply the answer from Step 1 by 100.

Step 3: You can round the number up or down to the nearest whole number or to one decimal place (1 dp). If the number ends in .49 or less, round it down. If it ends in .50 or more, round it up. So 15.37 would round to 15.4 per cent (1dp) or 15 per cent (to the nearest whole number).

Figure 1.17 Number of megacities (cities with a population greater than 10 million) in each continent

Continent	Number of megacities	
Africa	3	
Asia	China	15
	India	5
Rest of Asia	12	
Europe	3	
North America	3	
South America	5	
Total number	**46**	

15/46 = 0.32608

0.32608 × 100 = 32.608

= 32.6 (to 1dp)

12 Using Figure 1.17, calculate the percentage of all megacities in each of the following places. Show your answers to 1 dp.

a Rest of Asia

b India

c Europe

Calculating ratios

A **ratio** shows the relationship between one value and another. To find a ratio, you divide each term in the ratio by the same number. The life expectancy in the UK is 80 and in Congo is 60. You could be asked to calculate something like this in its simplest form.

We know that both numbers are divisible by 10, so that reduces our ratio to 8:6. Both numbers here are divisible by 2, so let's take the ratio down further to 4:3. There is no longer a number that is a multiple of either of those numbers, so the answer is **4:3**.

Longer, written response questions

These questions contain most of the AO2 marks and, for the higher-mark questions, there will also be AO3 marks awarded. This section shows you how to tackle smaller AO2 questions in a concise way as well as the depth required for longer 6- and 8-mark questions where you need to 'assess' or 'evaluate'. The student responses will help you learn how to structure your answers.

Use of case studies

Within the longer response questions ranging from 4 marks to 8 marks, you might be asked to draw upon your case study knowledge. There are ten official case studies within the OCR B specification. However, there are also many other places where you are expected to know some examples, such as the impacts of climate change on the UK.

At the start of Chapter 2 (page 19) and Chapter 3 (page 47), there is a table for you to complete with the case studies you have been taught and three place-specific facts – this means facts that are unique to that case study. Imagine if the examiner covered the space where you write the name of your case study. Could they still tell which case study you are writing about based on your facts related to that place?

> Case studies are detailed, located examples of the geography you have been taught. For example, you will have been taught about volcanic eruptions and Eyjafjallajökull is a case study of an eruption.

'Knowledge and understanding' questions

You will see many of the following questions that are testing AO1 (knowledge) and AO2 (understanding). The first question is purely an AO1 question as no explanations are required, just your knowledge.

> **13** Describe the soil found in Arctic areas. **3 marks**

Student answer

There is an **active upper layer** of the soil which freezes and unfreezes with seasonal changes in temperature. Below this, there is an area of **permafrost**: ground which has been frozen for two or more years. A layer known as **talik** is found beneath the permafrost.

> This question is point-marked, so you need to make three, clear observations about the soil in the Arctic. There is no need to explain why the soil is like this – that is not what the question is asking. Each point made in this answer includes a geographical word. This answer achieved the full 3 marks.

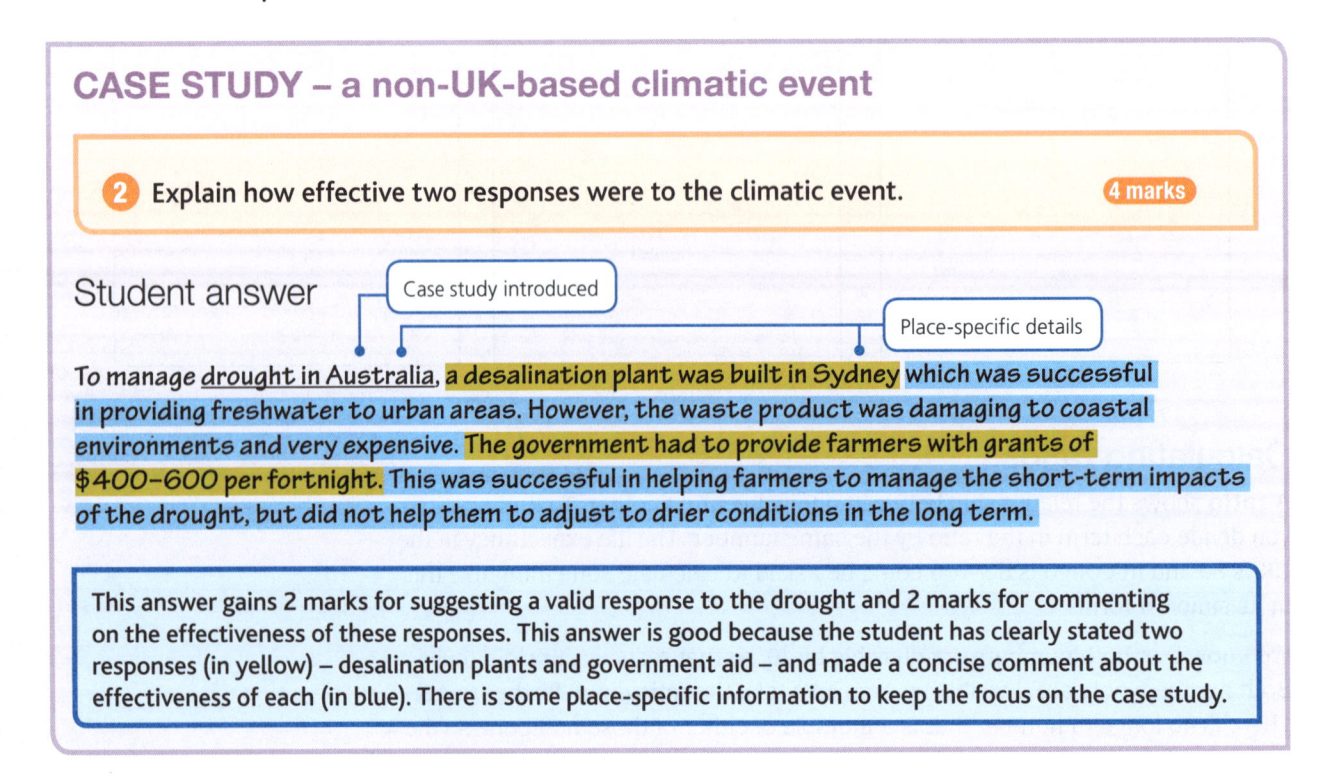

CASE STUDY – a non-UK-based climatic event

> **2** Explain how effective two responses were to the climatic event. **4 marks**

Student answer

Case study introduced / *Place-specific details*

To manage **drought in Australia**, **a desalination plant was built in Sydney** which was successful in providing freshwater to urban areas. However, the waste product was damaging to coastal environments and very expensive. **The government had to provide farmers with grants of $400–600 per fortnight.** This was successful in helping farmers to manage the short-term impacts of the drought, but did not help them to adjust to drier conditions in the long term.

> This answer gains 2 marks for suggesting a valid response to the drought and 2 marks for commenting on the effectiveness of these responses. This answer is good because the student has clearly stated two responses (in yellow) – desalination plants and government aid – and made a concise comment about the effectiveness of each (in blue). There is some place-specific information to keep the focus on the case study.

6-mark questions

You are most likely to have three 6-mark questions in Paper 1 and three 6-mark questions in Paper 2.

- These will always be at the end of topics and are likely to ask you to draw upon your knowledge and understanding (AO2) of a case study.
- The question will also test AO3 by asking you to 'discuss' or 'assess'.

Using PEEL

One way in which you can write a paragraph that is fully developed is to use the **PEEL** technique.

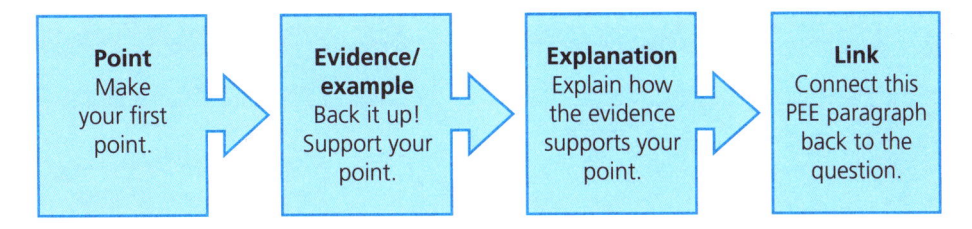

Point — Make your first point. → **Evidence/example** — Back it up! Support your point. → **Explanation** — Explain how the evidence supports your point. → **Link** — Connect this PEE paragraph back to the question.

Look at the student answer below to see their use of the PEEL technique.

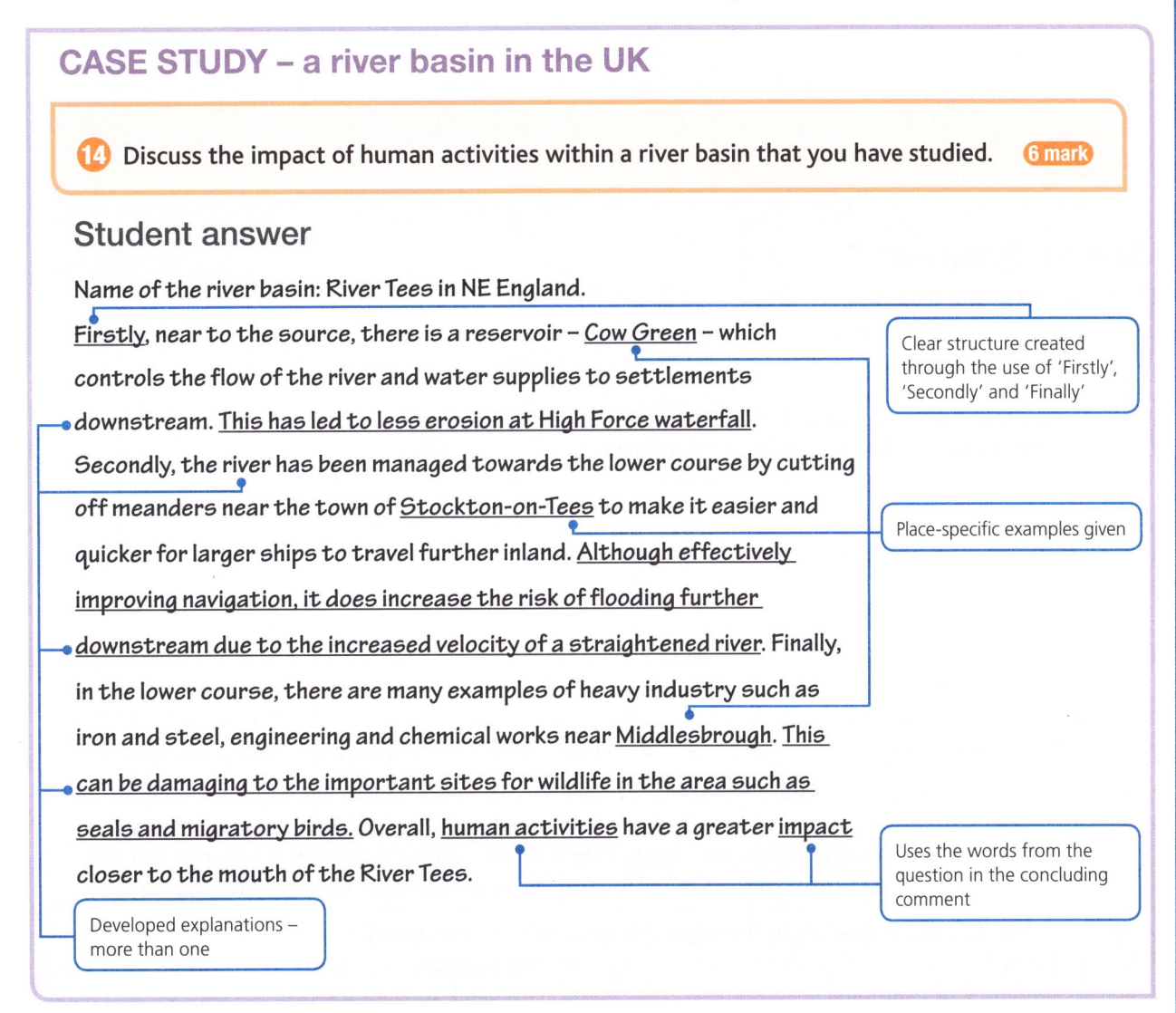

CASE STUDY – a river basin in the UK

14 Discuss the impact of human activities within a river basin that you have studied. **[6 mark]**

Student answer

Name of the river basin: River Tees in NE England.

Firstly, near to the source, there is a reservoir – Cow Green – which controls the flow of the river and water supplies to settlements downstream. This has led to less erosion at High Force waterfall. Secondly, the river has been managed towards the lower course by cutting off meanders near the town of Stockton-on-Tees to make it easier and quicker for larger ships to travel further inland. Although effectively improving navigation, it does increase the risk of flooding further downstream due to the increased velocity of a straightened river. Finally, in the lower course, there are many examples of heavy industry such as iron and steel, engineering and chemical works near Middlesbrough. This can be damaging to the important sites for wildlife in the area such as seals and migratory birds. Overall, human activities have a greater impact closer to the mouth of the River Tees.

Annotations:
- Clear structure created through the use of 'Firstly', 'Secondly' and 'Finally'
- Place-specific examples given
- Uses the words from the question in the concluding comment
- Developed explanations – more than one

Using the previous example as a model, answer the following question using a similar structure.

> **CASE STUDY – a coastal landscape in the UK**
>
> **15** Discuss the impact of human activities in a coastal landscape in the UK that you have studied. **6 marks**

....
....
....
....
....
....
....
....
....
....

'Assess' questions

The most frequent command word for the 6-mark question is 'assess'. Study the following example of a 6-mark question.

> **16** Assess the success of a small-scale example of sustainable management in either the Arctic or the Antarctic. **6 marks**

Read the student answer to the above exam question.

Student answer

Union Glacier is an expanse of ice where there is a camp which also has a natural runway where large cargo planes can land, bringing equipment for expeditions and scientific equipment. A crew set up the camp, laying fuel lines and putting up tents for the four months of the summer season. A small number of visitors explore the area and can do a variety of activities such as climbing, visiting penguin colonies and trekking.

Union Glacier is a mostly successful place because all of the waste is carefully contained and removed and some equipment is powered by solar panels. Furthermore, people who visit will return home with stories about a fragile environment which might make people think more carefully about climate change. However, machines such as the skidoos have to be powered by aviation fuel which might cause pollution in the area.

17 Use this PEEL technique key to highlight the student's answer above:
- Point
- Evidence or example
- Explanation
- Link back to the question

18 Now suggest two ways in which this answer could be improved.

1 ....

2 ....

8-mark questions

You will most likely have one 8-mark question in Section A of Paper 1 and another in Section A of Paper 2. This could appear at the end of any of the four topics. These questions will:
- test your ability to evaluate, looking at two sides of an argument, or to examine an issue in detail
- explore two assessment objectives: AO2 (understanding) and AO3 (making a judgement).

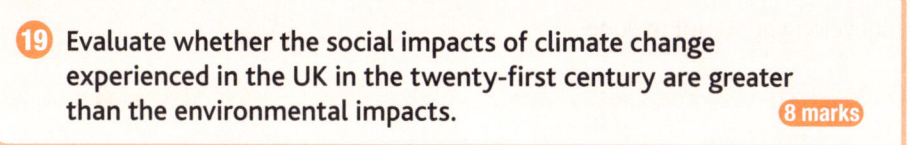

> **19** Evaluate whether the social impacts of climate change experienced in the UK in the twenty-first century are greater than the environmental impacts. **8 marks**

In this question, the two sides of the argument are **social impacts** and **environmental impacts** and the decision (or judgement) is **which impacts of climate change are worse** – social or environmental.

> **20** **Highlight** the following answer written by a GCSE Geography student to show where they have used elements of PEEL. Use different colours for each element of PEEL and complete the key below the student answer. Complete the table to note the strengths and weaknesses of this answer.
>
> ### Student answer
>
> Climate change in the UK will have many impacts. On average, the temperature will be hotter, meaning there will be more droughts in the south east regions. During the winter there will be more rain, meaning east coastal lowland is at risk of flooding along with the Teesside industries. Floods will also be more frequent and severe in places like Somerset. For crops, a hotter summer will mean new crops like peaches and oranges and an increased yield of crops like sugar, beet and wheat. The crops will also begin to move further north.
>
> Socially, a hotter summer means increased tourism in the Lake District, but the Cairngorm ski resorts will close due to lack of snow. The elderly will be at less risk of illnesses like flu during the winter, but more at risk of heatwave-related illness like heatstroke.
>
> Overall, I think it will have a greater impact environmentally as the natural disasters will increase, as will bird migration patterns and the flowering of crops, which will affect the country much more than tourism fluctuations.
>
> ☐ Point   ☐ Example
> ☐ Explanation   ☐ Link
>
> | Strengths of the answer | Weaknesses of the answer |
> |---|---|
> | | |

Using connectives to develop your understanding

The mark schemes refer to students writing 'well-developed' answers. You are far more likely to reach the top marks if you take one point and develop it as fully as you can rather than writing a lot of single ideas that are undeveloped.

The use of connectives will help you to write better answers that go into more depth. You can easily extend simple points by using connectives to link ideas. The most straightforward way to do this is to link one idea to the next with the phrase 'which means that...'. In order to think about how to extend simple points, you can also ask yourself: 'So what?'

Other useful phrases to help to develop your point include:
- Furthermore...
- Additionally...
- As a result of this...
- Consequently...

21 Complete the other developed ideas in Figure 1.18 by explaining the remaining three points.

Point	Explanation	Further explanation
There are more opportunities for employment in urban areas...	...which means that there is a better chance of getting a higher wage.	As a result of this, people are likely to be able to spend money on services, improving their quality of life.
The housing is of a better quality...	...which means that...	As a result of this,...
The healthcare system is better...		
Cities become transport hubs...		

Figure 1.18 Using connectives to turn simple points into developed ideas. Pull factors that encourage people into urban areas in LIDCs

How to 'assess' and 'evaluate' – the Extent-o-meter

For the longer-answer questions worth 6 or 8 marks, you are often required to weigh up two sides of an argument by considering **how far** you agree or disagree with the question or statement. Similarly, you might need to assess whether the advantages are **greater than** the disadvantages or whether, for example, social impacts **outweigh** economic impacts.

These questions carry AO3 marks, which means that you need to apply your knowledge and understanding of geography to reach a judgement and/or conclusion. To do this, your answers need to move beyond simple recall of your case study knowledge.

To help you to achieve this, consider where your judgement would be on a 'to what extent...' or 'how far...' scale such as the 'Extent-o-meter' shown in Figure 1.19.

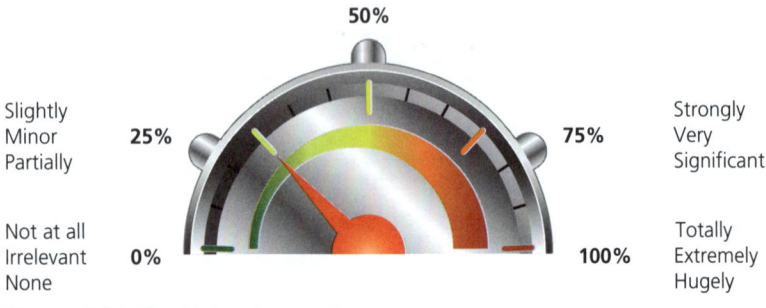

Slightly / Minor / Partially — 25%
50%
Strongly / Very / Significant — 75%
Not at all / Irrelevant / None — 0%
Totally / Extremely / Hugely — 100%

Figure 1.19 The Extent-o-meter

The following phrases are possible sentence starters that you might use in an answer.
- In conclusion, I **partially** agree that...
- Overall, the social impacts are **slightly** more **significant** than the economic impacts because...
- The statement is **not at all** true because...
- ...is **very** sustainable because...

Chapter 2 Preparing for Paper 1: Our Natural World

Remember that this paper contains all of your physical geography questions and covers the following four topics:

- Global hazards
- Changing climate
- Distinctive landscapes
- Sustaining ecosystems

On pages 19–46 you will practise some of the questions for Paper 1. There is a variety of question styles ranging from 1-mark 'define' or 'calculate' questions through to more challenging 6- and 8-mark 'assess' and 'evaluate' questions. Use the exam advice and activities to support you through the questions.

As well as the practice questions, it is important to remind yourself of the case studies you would expect to see coming up in each topic for the longer-response questions. You are likely to be going into the exam wondering which case studies will come up, as well as having your AO1 knowledge facts stored in your memory.

Use of case studies

Remember that most questions asking you to use your knowledge of case studies will be indicated by the words **CASE STUDY** in capital letters and bold print to help you to spot them easily. Most importantly, you need to be able to identify **which** case study is needed for each of these questions.

> 1. Complete the table on page 20 with the case studies that you have been taught as part of your GCSE Geography course for Paper 1 and give three place-specific facts about each case study. Although the changing climate topic does not have a specific case study, the specification does say that you need to know about both worldwide and UK impacts of climate change, so you can add these into the table here.
>
> 2. Read the following 6-mark questions and write next to them which case study you think you would need to use. This is the same process you should go through in the real exam. Take some time to work out which case study you are being asked to use. It can be very easy to mix them up by mistake and lose out on valuable marks.

CASE STUDY – a tectonic event

1. Assess the social and economic consequences of a tectonic event you have studied. **6 marks**

CASE STUDY – a coastal landscape in the UK

2. Discuss the geomorphic processes involved in the formation of a coastal landform. **6 marks**

CASE STUDY – a small-scale example of sustainable management

3. Assess the sustainability of a small scale attempt to manage the Arctic or Antarctic. **6 marks**

Topic	Case study required	Your case study	Three place-specific facts
Global hazards — For the weather hazard, you must have an example of: • a flash flood OR a tropical storm • a heatwave OR a drought	UK-based weather hazard		1 2 3
	Non-UK-based weather hazard		1 2 3
	A tectonic event		1 2 3
Changing climate	Worldwide impacts of climate change		1 2 3
	UK impacts of climate change		1 2 3
Distinctive landscapes	UK coastal landscape		1 2 3
	UK river basin		1 2 3
Sustaining ecosystems	Sustainable management of an area of tropical rainforest at a local or regional scale		1 2 3
	Small-scale example of sustainable management in the Arctic or Antarctic		1 2 3
	Global example of sustainable management in the Arctic or Antarctic		1 2 3

Topic 1: Global Hazards

Exam practice questions

1 Name **two** conditions needed for a tropical storm to form. *2 marks*

1. a lot of heat to form and sea surface temperature of at least 26°
2. between 5 and 20° north or south of the equator

> Although 2-mark questions do not need to be fully developed answers, ensure that your answer is technically accurate. For example, rather than writing 'the water needs to be warm', quote the temperature required. Instead of writing 'the water needs to be deep enough', state how deep.

2 Define the term air pressure. *1 mark*

the force exerted on a surface by the air above it as gravity pulls it to Earth.

3 Define the term convection current. *1 mark*

Heat rising and falling inside the mantle creates connection currents generated by radioactive decay in the core.

4 Define the term hotspot. *1 mark*

an area on earth over a mantle plume or an area under the rocky outer layers of Earth, called the crust, where magma is hotter than surrounding magma.

5 Suggest **two** ways in which governments could mitigate the impacts of earthquakes. *2 marks*

providing education on earthquake safety.
building safer structures.

> This is an easy question to get wrong due to the range of key words used. Remember how useful it is to BUG a question (see page 4).

6 Suggest **two** ways in which governments could mitigate the impacts of earthquakes. *2 marks*

- Simply state/name them – no complicated descriptions needed
- Make sure you focus on earthquakes and not strategies used with volcanic eruptions
- Consider policies and laws that the government could put in place
- Mitigate means to reduce the impacts of a hazard (this is not about prediction)

Sidebar notes:

Make sure that you include enough in your definition to secure the mark available. Some students give a very basic definition, which means that they struggle to achieve the mark available. Remember to use good geographical vocabulary when you are writing definitions.

In the example here, consider WHAT air pressure is and HOW it is measured.

Try to include all of the following terms in your definition of convection currents: mantle, core, crust, current, radioactive decay, heating, cooling.

Try to include all of the following terms in your definition of a hotspot: plume, magma, crust, oceanic plate, thin, fracture.

7 Explain how volcanoes are created at destructive margins. *4 marks*

The plate melts after the subduction zone, due to friction, it become molten rock (magma). The magma then forces its way up to the side of the plate boundary to form a volcano

> Think about question 7 as a series of stages. The following words and phrases will help you to write your answer:
> - Oceanic and continental plate
> - Friction as the plate subducts
> - Melting oceanic plate
> - Increasing pressure
> - Magma rising
> - Composite (strato) volcano

You can adapt questions from this workbook to make your own new questions! For example, you could change the question above to 'Explain how **earthquakes** are created at **conservative** margins'.

CASE STUDY – a tectonic event

4 Discuss the consequences of your chosen tectonic event on people and the economy. *6 marks*

> Before you write your answer, create a mind map in your notebook of the consequences of the tectonic event you have studied.
>
> Now colour code the consequences using the following key:
> - Social (affected people)
> - Economic (affected jobs and money)
> - Environmental (affects the natural landscape).
>
> Were some of the consequences short-term (days/weeks) or long-term (months/years)?

22

8 Between which circulation cells is the temperate climate found?

1 mark

- a Hadley and Hadley ☐
- c Ferrel and Polar ☐
- b Hadley and Ferrel ☐
- d Polar and Hadley ☐

9 Describe the weather conditions found where the two Hadley cells meet.

3 marks

....
....
....
....
....

10 Explain how El Niño causes droughts.

4 marks

....
....
....
....
....
....

> El Niño is a weather phenomenon that happens in the Pacific Ocean, bringing droughts to Australia and floods to South America.
>
> Use the following statements in your answer. Be careful, though: they are not in the correct order.
> - Less air rising
> - Trade winds weaken
> - Warm dry weather
> - Warm water travels eastwards
> - Water becomes cooler
> - High pressure

11 Suggest why tectonic plates move.

3 marks

....
....
....
....
....

Sketch the global circulation system in the space below.

Now read question 9 again and use your sketch to help you.

Question 9 is a great AO2 question as you need to show that you can apply your knowledge of the cells to demonstrate an understanding of how they affect the weather.

Refer back to your sketch of the global circulation system. Ask yourself:
- Where do the Hadley cells meet?
- What do you know about the ecosystem that exists there?
- Is it a high- or low-pressure area?
- What would the weather be like?

Figure 2.1 Largest worldwide earthquakes over the last ten years

Year	Magnitude	Death toll	Location
2018	8.2	0	Fiji
2017	8.2	98	Mexico
2016	7.8	676	Ecuador
2015	8.3	14	Chile
2014	8.2	6	Chile
2013	8.3	0	Russia
2012	8.6	10	Indonesia
2011	9.1	20896	Japan
2010	8.8	525	Chile
2009	8.1	192	Samoa

12a Select the most suitable graphical technique for presenting the magnitude of the earthquakes. *(1 mark)*

   a Line graph ☐   c Histogram ☐
   b Bar graph ☐   d Radar graph ☐

Refer back to page 10 to help you decide which graphical technique would be the most suitable.

12b Calculate the median of the death tolls. Show your workings. *(2 marks)*

Use the space here to write the death tolls in order from the smallest to the highest figure.

12c Calculate the lower quartile. Show your workings. *(2 marks)*

Use your list to show how you would calculate the lower quartile. Use Figure 1.15 on page 12 as a model.

13 Name two features of a shield volcano. *(2 marks)*

   1 ....

   2 ....

In question 13, you get 1 mark for each feature that you identify. Shield volcanoes are often found in the hotspot location of Hawaii.

Make sure you do not confuse the features of a shield volcano with those of a strato volcano.

CASE STUDY – a UK-based weather hazard event

5 Assess the significance of the causes of your chosen event. *(6 marks)*

Complete this answer in your notebook.

You need three PEEL paragraphs here:
1. *The most significant cause*
2. *A fairly significant cause*
3. *The least significant cause*

Topic 2: Changing Climate

Exam practice questions

14 Which of the following is a significant source of the greenhouse gas methane? *1 mark*

- a Vehicle exhausts ☐
- b Burning fossil fuels ☐
- c Livestock and rice cultivation ☐
- d Deforestation ☐

> For multiple choice questions, remember to use a 'process of elimination'.
>
> Consider:
> - Which sources do you definitely know are NOT sources of methane? You can eliminate (remove) them from the list.
> - Which other greenhouse gas might some of them emit rather than methane?
> - What are you left with?

15 Explain how volcanic eruptions can cause natural climate change. *3 marks*

Before you write your own answer, look at how this student has used PEE.

Student answer

Volcanic eruptions send huge quantities of ash, gases and liquids into the atmosphere, *[Point: state the cause]*

which can block the sun, leading to a reduction in surface temperatures. *[Explain the impact it has on climate change]*

This was evidenced by the eruption of Mount Pinatubo in Indonesia in 1991 where the ash and gases, including sulphur dioxide, cooled the world's temperatures by up to 1.3°C for three years. *[Give an example]*

16 Explain how sunspots can cause natural climate change. *3 marks*

17 Explain how sea level rise is likely to affect low-lying coastal areas. *3 marks*

This student has used the PEE method:

Student answer

People who live near the coast will have to move from their homes. *[Point]*

This might mean moving further inland, or for small low-lying islands, this might mean to a different country. *[Explanation/Development]*

An example of this is the island of Kiribati in the Pacific Ocean from which some residents have already moved to New Zealand. *[Example]*

Choose a different point to write your own answer to question 17 using PEE.

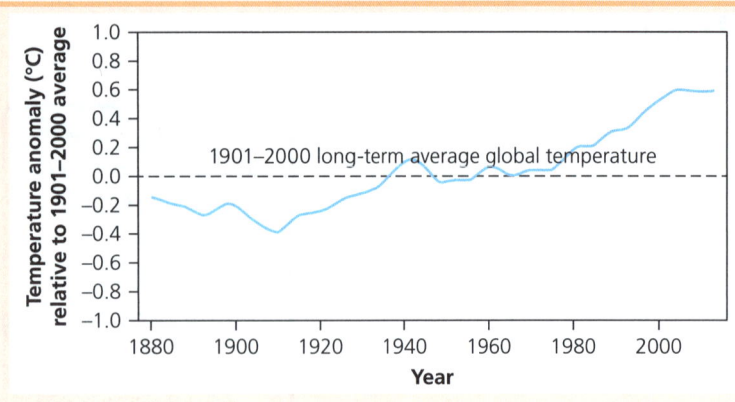

Figure 2.2 Long-term average global temperatures, 1880–2013

18 Using data from Figure 2.2, describe the average global temperature change from 1880 to 2013.

4 marks

Fill in the gaps to help you practise this type of answer.

The average global temperatures have generally .... from 1880–2013. It was 0.18 below the 1901–2000 average in 1880 and increased to .... above the average in 2000. There were a couple of exceptions in .... and .... when the temperatures decreased.

Question 18 is ideal for using the GCSE structure:

G = General

C = Comment (is the trend increasing/ decreasing/ fluctuating?)

S = Specific data (show that you can read the graph by using numbers)

E = Exceptions (also known as anomalies – mention something which does not fit the pattern)

This is a point-marked question:

1 mark = describing the trend

1 mark = making specific points

1 mark = use of data

1 mark = communicating in a logical order

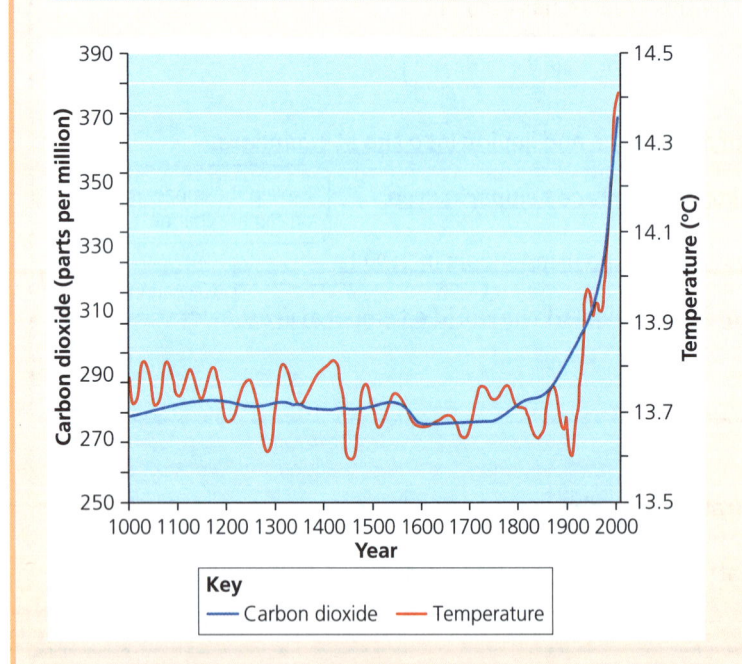

Figure 2.3 Carbon dioxide and global temperature change

19 Using data from Figure 2.3, describe the changes in global temperature from 1000 to 2000.

4 marks

Use the GCSE structure to write your own response to question 19.

20 Discuss the reliability of at least two sources of evidence for climate change.

6 marks

Use the structure strip to complete your answer.

- The first source of evidence is …

- This source can measure climate change up to …………………… years ago.
  It is measured by …

- It suggests the climate has changed because …

- This source is completely/partially/not very reliable because …

- The second source of evidence is …

- This source can measure climate change up to …………………… years ago.
  It is measured by …

- It suggests the climate has changed because …

- This source is completely/partially/not very reliable because …

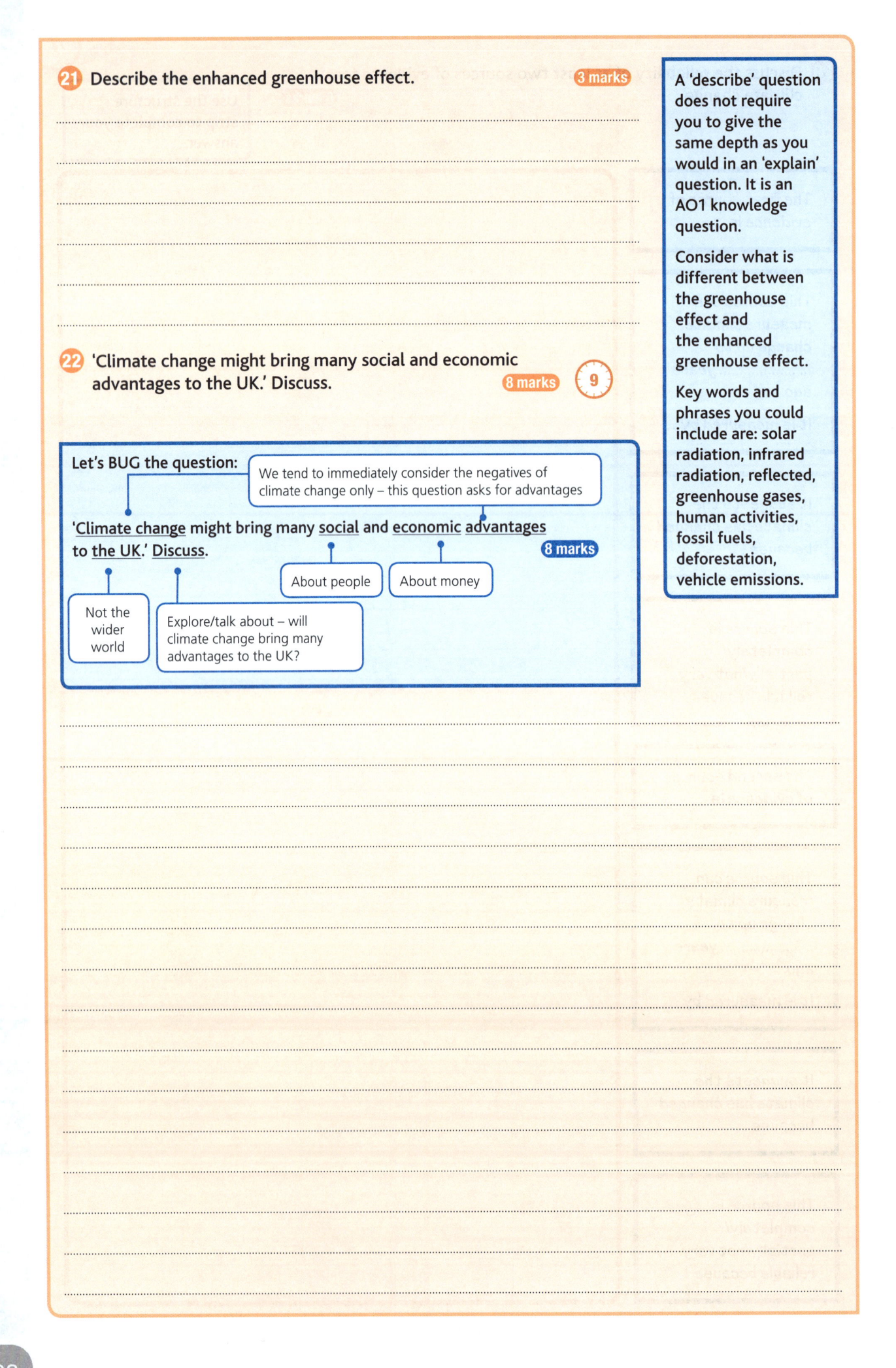

21 Describe the enhanced greenhouse effect. 3 marks

> A 'describe' question does not require you to give the same depth as you would in an 'explain' question. It is an AO1 knowledge question.
>
> Consider what is different between the greenhouse effect and the enhanced greenhouse effect.
>
> Key words and phrases you could include are: solar radiation, infrared radiation, reflected, greenhouse gases, human activities, fossil fuels, deforestation, vehicle emissions.

22 'Climate change might bring many social and economic advantages to the UK.' Discuss. 8 marks

Let's BUG the question:

'Climate change might bring many social and economic advantages to the UK.' Discuss. 8 marks

- We tend to immediately consider the negatives of climate change only – this question asks for advantages
- About people
- About money
- Not the wider world
- Explore/talk about – will climate change bring many advantages to the UK?

28

Topic 3: Distinctive Landscapes

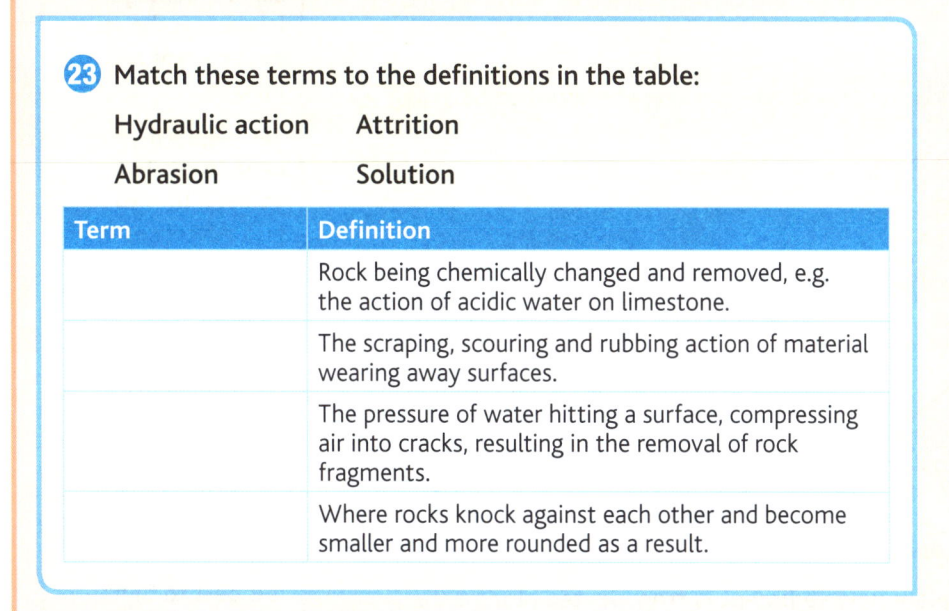

23 Match these terms to the definitions in the table:

Hydraulic action   Attrition

Abrasion   Solution

Term	Definition
	Rock being chemically changed and removed, e.g. the action of acidic water on limestone.
	The scraping, scouring and rubbing action of material wearing away surfaces.
	The pressure of water hitting a surface, compressing air into cracks, resulting in the removal of rock fragments.
	Where rocks knock against each other and become smaller and more rounded as a result.

> Knowing the four processes of erosion and how they affect both the coast and rivers is essential. You will also need to apply these words in longer-answer questions.
>
> There are four processes: hydraulic action, attrition, abrasion and solution.
>
> Complete the activity to revise these terms.

Exam practice questions

24 Describe how hydraulic action erodes the coast. **2 marks**

25 Describe how abrasion causes erosion in rivers. **2 marks**

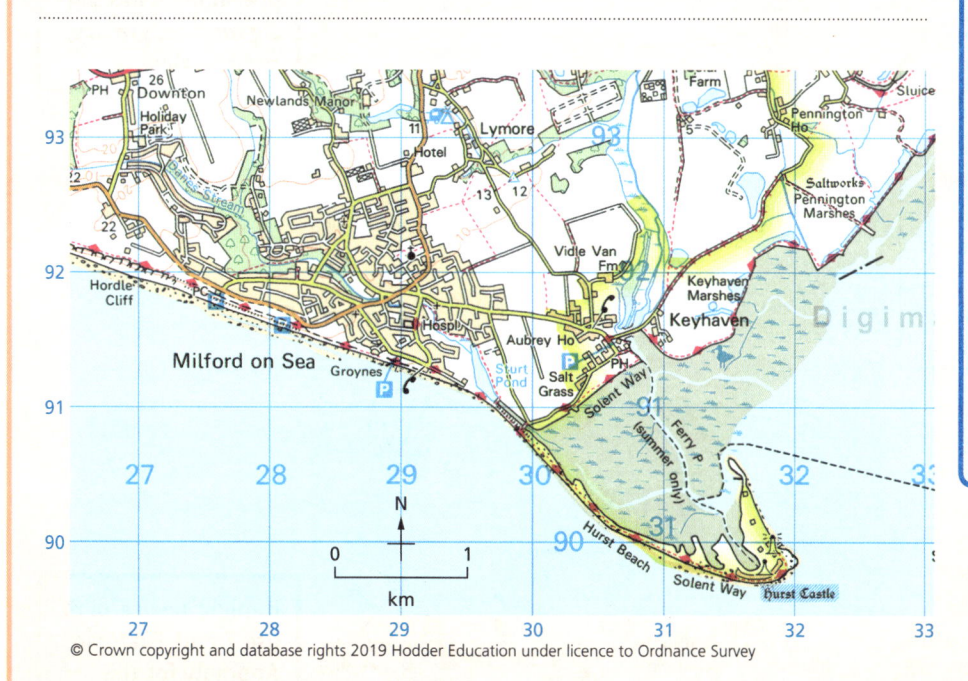

> For questions 24 and 25, use 'read, cover, write, check' to complete the two exam questions.
>
> **Step 1:** Read the key words and definitions in activity 23.
>
> **Step 2:** Cover the key words and definitions.
>
> **Step 3:** Write your answer to questions 24 and 25.
>
> **Step 4:** Check whether you missed anything from the definitions. Is it clear from your definitions that you have responded to the words 'coast' and 'rivers' in your answer?

Figure 2.4 OS map of a coastal landscape

26 Name the coastal landform shown in Figure 2.4. **1 mark**

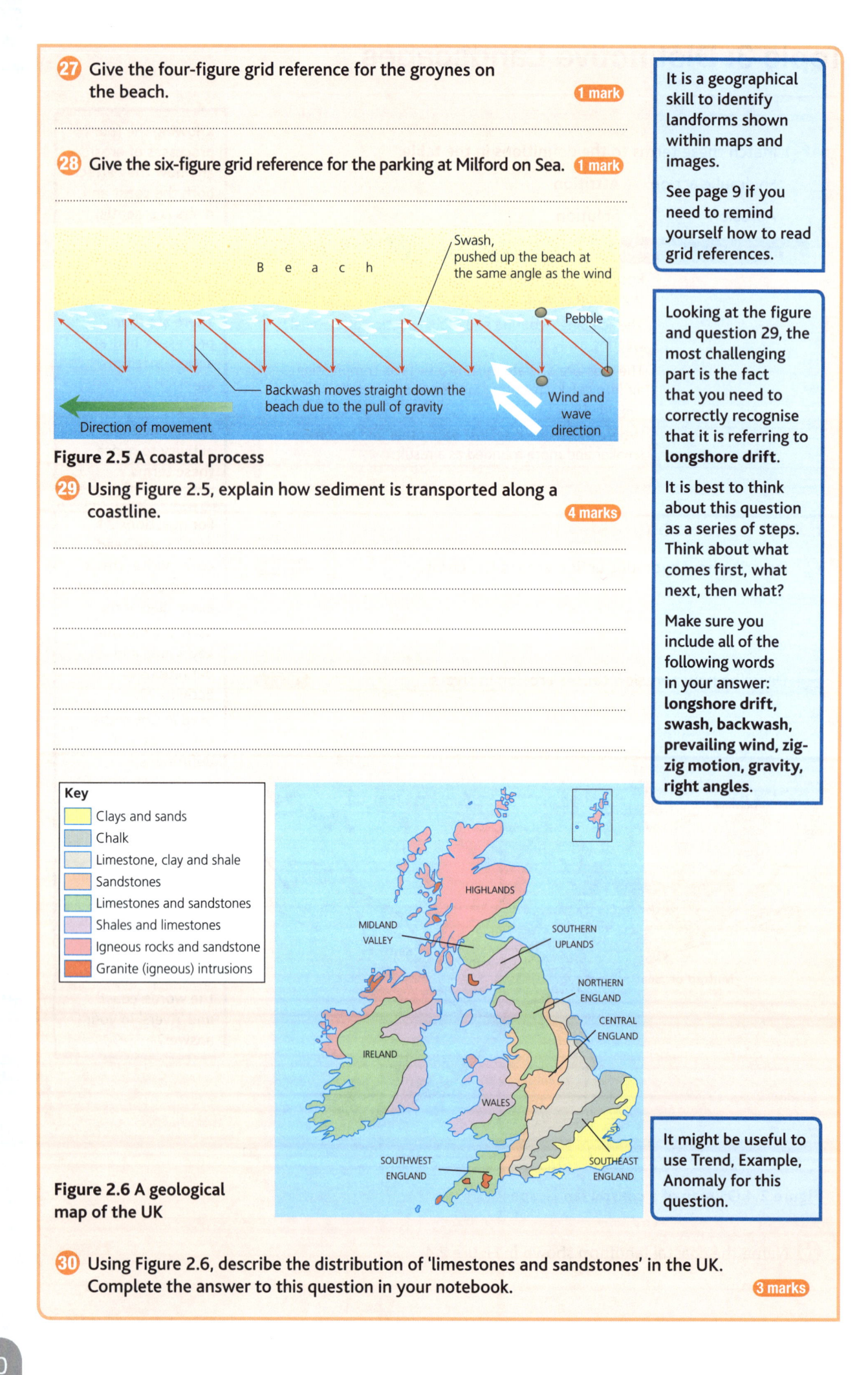

27 Give the four-figure grid reference for the groynes on the beach. `1 mark`

....

28 Give the six-figure grid reference for the parking at Milford on Sea. `1 mark`

....

It is a geographical skill to identify landforms shown within maps and images.

See page 9 if you need to remind yourself how to read grid references.

Figure 2.5 A coastal process

29 Using Figure 2.5, explain how sediment is transported along a coastline. `4 marks`

....
....
....
....
....
....

*Looking at the figure and question 29, the most challenging part is the fact that you need to correctly recognise that it is referring to **longshore drift**.*

It is best to think about this question as a series of steps. Think about what comes first, what next, then what?

*Make sure you include all of the following words in your answer: **longshore drift, swash, backwash, prevailing wind, zig-zig motion, gravity, right angles.***

Figure 2.6 A geological map of the UK

Key
- Clays and sands
- Chalk
- Limestone, clay and shale
- Sandstones
- Limestones and sandstones
- Shales and limestones
- Igneous rocks and sandstone
- Granite (igneous) intrusions

It might be useful to use Trend, Example, Anomaly for this question.

30 Using Figure 2.6, describe the distribution of 'limestones and sandstones' in the UK. Complete the answer to this question in your notebook. `3 marks`

31 Match the four processes of transportation in rivers to the correct definition below:

Traction   Saltation
Suspension   Solution

Key word	Definition
	Where very fine, light material is carried along in the flow of the water.
	Small pebbles and stones bounce along the river bed.
	Some minerals in sediment are dissolved in the water.
	Large boulders and rocks are rolled along the river bed.

32 Explain **two** ways in which a river transports its load. **4 marks**

> In question 32, you would get 1 mark for naming a process and another mark for explaining how it works. As it is a 4-mark question, you need to ensure that you have done this twice!

Figure 2.7 Hunstanton Cliffs, Norfolk

33 Suggest how the coastline shown in Figure 2.7 might be affected by weathering. **3 marks**

> Question 33 is worth 3 marks so you need to make three separate points.
>
> Don't be tempted to write everything you know about weathering. Your answer must be based on the evidence in the figure.
>
> Possible answer structure: This coastline is affected by...weathering because [say what you see in the source as evidence]. It could also be affected by...weathering because...

Chapter 2 Preparing for Paper 1: Our Natural World

CASE STUDY – the landscape of a UK river basin

6 Discuss how geomorphic processes have contributed to the formation of a landform within your chosen river basin.

6 marks

Read the following basic response from a student discussing the formation of High Force Waterfall on the River Tees in North East England. It does not include any geographical words or place-specific detail.

Student answer

High Force Waterfall was created when rock type along the river changed. The river goes over hard rock and wears away the soft rock. This makes a ledge over which the water goes. As the river continues to wear away the soft rock, it creates a deep pool of water at the bottom. Eventually, the hard rock above cannot be supported and it falls into the water. The material at the base of the waterfall makes the pool deeper and the material becomes so small that it is carried away. This keeps happening and the waterfall moves backwards.

Using Figure 2.8 to help you, rewrite the answer in the space provided, remembering to use key geographical words and place-specific details.

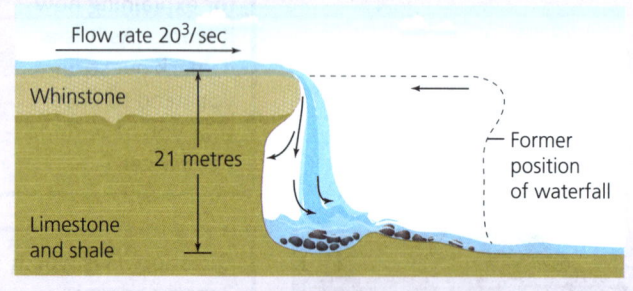

Figure 2.8 The formation of High Force Waterfall

34 Which of these statements is true? — **1 mark**

a   The velocity is fastest on the inside of a meander ☐
b   A river cliff forms on the inside of a meander ☐
c   The depth of the river is greater on the outside of a meander ☐
d   Deposition occurs on the outside of a meander ☐

> To help you consider which statement above is true, draw and annotate a cross-section of a meander in the space below.
>
> **Cross-section:** shows the shape of a feature (such as a mountain or meander) viewed from the side as if it were cut through with a knife.

35 Explain the formation of a V-shaped valley. — **3 marks**

> To help answer question 35, organise the following statements into the correct order to explain the formation of a V-shaped valley:
> - This leaves a steep-sided and narrow valley shape.
> - The valley sides are slowly broken down through weathering.
> - In the upper course, the river only has enough energy to erode downwards.
> - Weathered material is transported via gravity and rainfall towards the river channel.

....
....
....
....

36 Suggest one difference between an upland and a lowland area. — **1 mark**

....
....

> For question 36, you need one clear sentence for this answer. The connective 'whereas' would be useful to connect the two points about an upland and a lowland area.
>
> Upland areas are…whereas lowland areas are…

Chapter 2 Preparing for Paper 1: Our Natural World

33

CASE STUDY – a coastal landscape in the UK

7 Discuss how human activity works with geomorphic process to impact the coastal landscape you have studied.

Case study: ....

6 marks

First, look at how you can BUG the question, then read the student's answer below and note their use of PEEL. Then you can complete your own answer to the question, using your case study in your notebook.

Decide the importance of how <u>human activity</u> works with <u>geomorphic processes</u> to impact the coastal landscape you have studied.

6 marks

- Could include industries such as tourism and how people manage the coastline
- Include processes of erosion, transportation and deposition

Student answer using PEEL

CASE STUDY – Dawlish Warren, Devon

Point: A new sea wall was constructed in 1993 to protect the valuable tourist shops and facilities on the warren. Tourism is the area's main source of income and it is a popular destination for holidaymakers in the summer. **Evidence:** The sea wall was expensive at £5000 per metre but **Explanation:** is effective at holding the line and protecting the coastline from erosion. **Link:** It has reduced the processes of erosion in this location, leading to less deposition further along the spit.

Topic 4: Sustaining Ecosystems

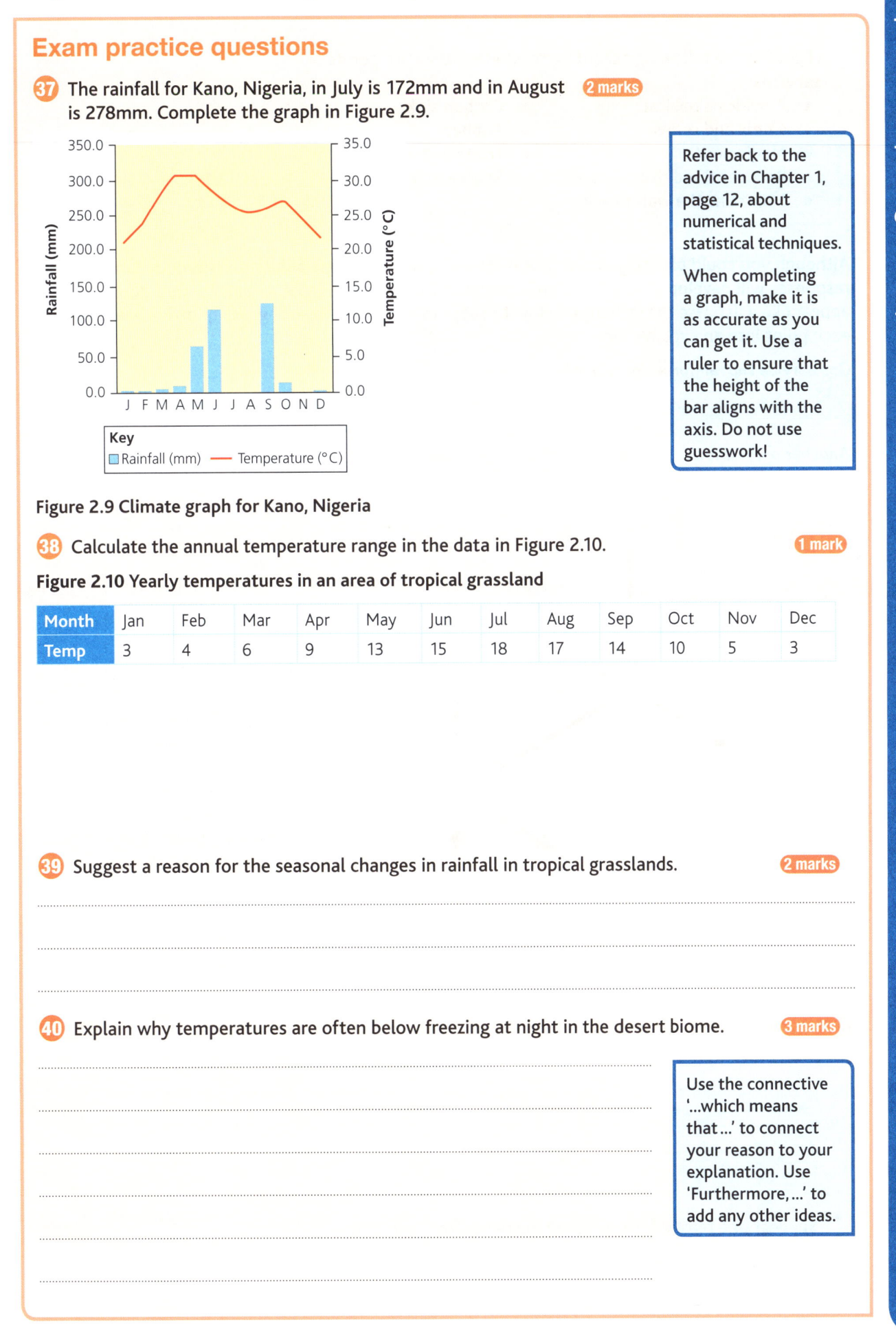

Exam practice questions

37 The rainfall for Kano, Nigeria, in July is 172mm and in August is 278mm. Complete the graph in Figure 2.9. **2 marks**

> Refer back to the advice in Chapter 1, page 12, about numerical and statistical techniques.
>
> When completing a graph, make it is as accurate as you can get it. Use a ruler to ensure that the height of the bar aligns with the axis. Do not use guesswork!

Figure 2.9 Climate graph for Kano, Nigeria

38 Calculate the annual temperature range in the data in Figure 2.10. **1 mark**

Figure 2.10 Yearly temperatures in an area of tropical grassland

Month	Jan	Feb	Mar	Apr	May	Jun	Jul	Aug	Sep	Oct	Nov	Dec
Temp	3	4	6	9	13	15	18	17	14	10	5	3

39 Suggest a reason for the seasonal changes in rainfall in tropical grasslands. **2 marks**

....
....
....

40 Explain why temperatures are often below freezing at night in the desert biome. **3 marks**

....
....

> Use the connective '…which means that…' to connect your reason to your explanation. Use 'Furthermore,…' to add any other ideas.

....
....

41 Explain two services that the tropical rainforest provides. `4 marks`

> Highlight the following according to whether they are **goods** or **services**:
> - Provides a habitat
> - Gums and resins
> - Medicines
> - Reduces flood risk
> - Maintains the water cycle
> - Carbon sink
> - Rubber
> - Fruits and vegetables
> - Source of income

Although you could probably access 3 or 4 marks by making single points for this question, the best responses will develop a 'point' into an 'explanation' in order to create an answer that does not appear like a list. Use the structure below to support you with answering this question. Develop each point into an explanation.

One service the rainforest provides is………………………………………………………………………………………………………

………

Another service is………

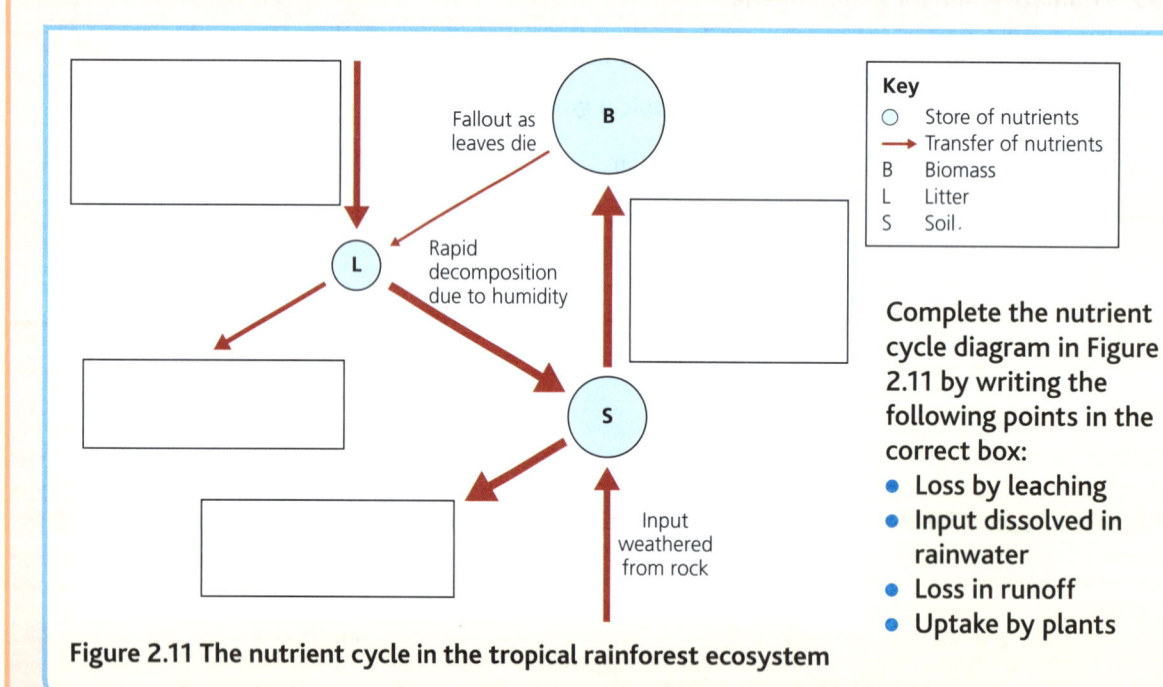

………

Key
- ○ Store of nutrients
- → Transfer of nutrients
- B Biomass
- L Litter
- S Soil.

Complete the nutrient cycle diagram in Figure 2.11 by writing the following points in the correct box:
- Loss by leaching
- Input dissolved in rainwater
- Loss in runoff
- Uptake by plants

Figure 2.11 The nutrient cycle in the tropical rainforest ecosystem

42 Why is the litter layer the smallest store of nutrients in the tropical rainforest? `2 marks`

………

………

………

43 Suggest one reason for the loss of nutrients from the soil. `1 mark`

………

………

44 Evaluate the role that human activities have had on the exploitation of the tropical rainforest.

8 marks

This is an example of a question that does **not** ask you to use one of your case studies, but it is still worth 8 marks. Although it is not a 'case study question', being able to name examples will give greater depth to your answer.

a Don't forget to BUG the question! Refer back to page 4 in Chapter 1 to remind you of the technique.

b List the possible human activities you **could** include. You should be able to name at least **six** human activities.

c For each human activity you have listed, consider how much it exploits (takes advantage of) the rainforest and mark it on the continuum line below with a cross and a label.

Little impact on the rainforest — Big impact on the rainforest

d Now, read the student answer below and add two further paragraphs of your own choosing from your continuum. Continue your answer in your notebook.

Student answer: sample PEEL paragraph

Mining for minerals such as gold, copper and diamonds exploits the rainforest. — **Point**

Local communities are displaced from their land and experience contamination of the soil and water supplies. — **Evidence**

An example of these communities is found in Peru, South America. The country is the world's second highest producer of zinc. — **Explanation**

Although it could be argued that the money made from mining helps to fund infrastructure, such as roads and electricity, people are affected by contaminated water and soil. — **Link**

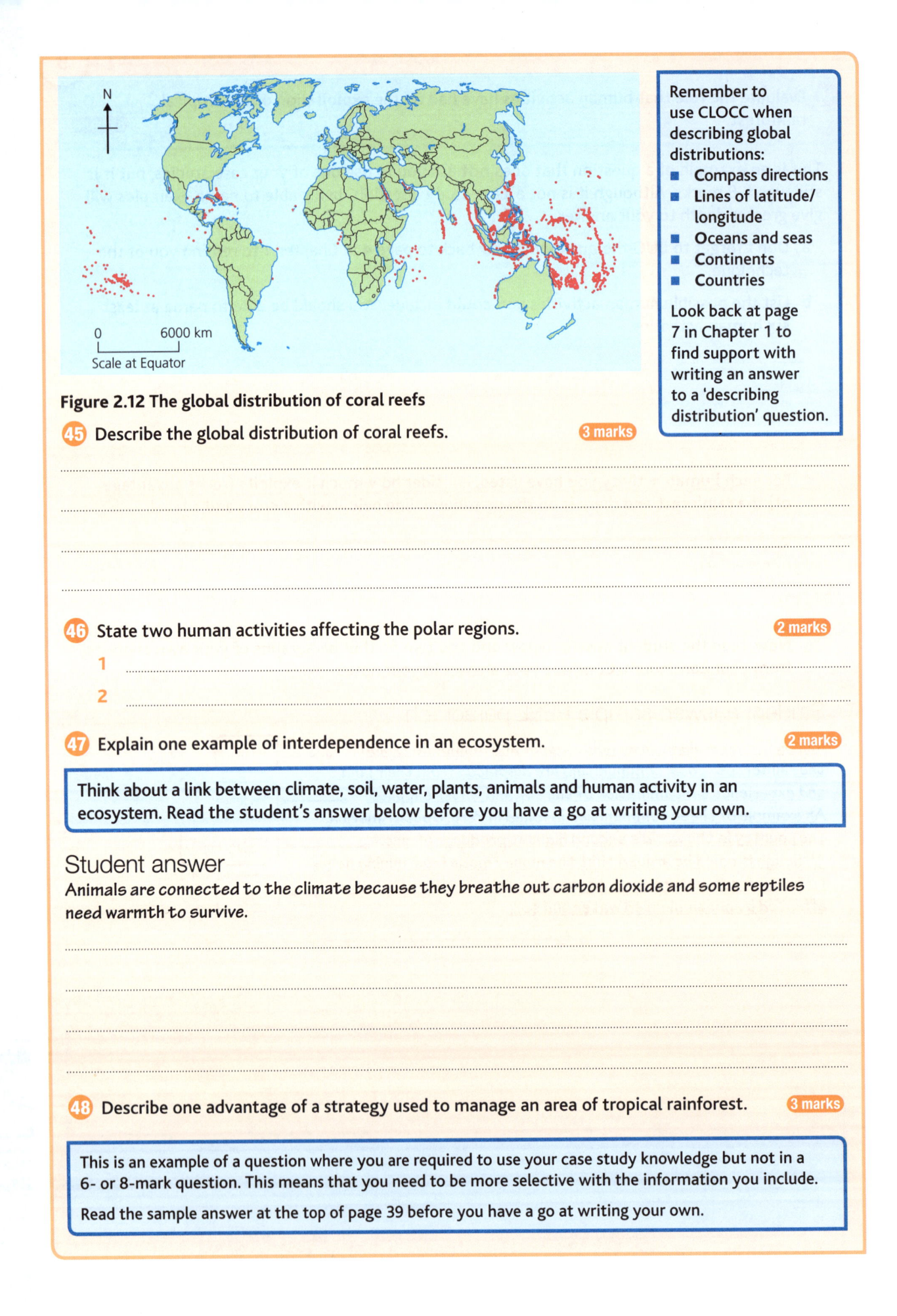

Figure 2.12 The global distribution of coral reefs

> Remember to use CLOCC when describing global distributions:
> - **Compass directions**
> - **Lines of latitude/longitude**
> - **Oceans and seas**
> - **Continents**
> - **Countries**
>
> Look back at page 7 in Chapter 1 to find support with writing an answer to a 'describing distribution' question.

45 Describe the global distribution of coral reefs. **3 marks**

....
....
....
....

46 State two human activities affecting the polar regions. **2 marks**

1 ....
2 ....

47 Explain one example of interdependence in an ecosystem. **2 marks**

> Think about a link between climate, soil, water, plants, animals and human activity in an ecosystem. Read the student's answer below before you have a go at writing your own.

Student answer
Animals are connected to the climate because they breathe out carbon dioxide and some reptiles need warmth to survive.

....
....
....
....

48 Describe one advantage of a strategy used to manage an area of tropical rainforest. **3 marks**

> This is an example of a question where you are required to use your case study knowledge but not in a 6- or 8-mark question. This means that you need to be more selective with the information you include.
>
> Read the sample answer at the top of page 39 before you have a go at writing your own.

Sample answer
In the Monteverde Cloud Forest of Costa Rica, where ecotourism is used to sustainably manage the rainforest, the money made from tourism is invested back into the local community through schools and community projects. This means that local people's literacy levels and their quality of life improve.

....

....

....

....

....

49 Evaluate the success of a global example of sustainable management in either the Arctic or Antarctica. **8 marks** ⏱ 9

Let's BUG the question:

<u>Evaluate</u> the <u>success</u> of a <u>global</u> example of sustainable management in either <u>the Arctic</u> or <u>Antarctica</u>.

- Weigh up – to what extent is it successful?
- You need to use your global example, not a small-scale example
- Examples could include the Antarctic Treaty or Earth Summits
- Don't write about both poles!

8 marks

Add your case study information as annotations onto the continuum below. Decide the extent to which it is a successful or unsuccessful aspect of the case study.

Not Successful •————————————————————————————————• Very Successful

Now write your answer in full in your notebook. You will need to include a conclusion which clearly states the extent to which you think your chosen example has been successful. Use the language of the extent-o-meter on page 18 to help you.

Section B: Physical geography fieldwork

In the fieldwork section of Paper 1, you will be given mostly AO4 (skills) questions that ask you to, for example:
- use statistics to analyse fieldwork data
- suggest appropriate ways to present data
- state primary and secondary methods of data collection.

You will also be asked an 8-mark question at the end of the paper either about the fieldwork you carried out or about fieldwork results contained in the Resource Booklet. In either case, you will be asked to explore any area of the enquiry process, such as:
- Discuss and evaluate fieldwork techniques.
- Reach a conclusion to the fieldwork.
- Discuss how your enquiry question helped you to understand more about the geographical issue.

This chapter gives you the opportunity to practise questions on both your own fieldwork and unfamiliar fieldwork.

> You should have completed a fieldwork experience in a physical environment (e.g. along a river, at a coastal landscape). To help you to organise your fieldwork notes, complete the questions over these two pages. The activities take you sequentially through the fieldwork process, from deciding on your question to reaching a conclusion. You will need to use your notebook to complete these tasks in detail.

My fieldwork record

1 Route to enquiry

a Location and date of fieldwork:

....

....

b Enquiry question:

....

....

> The exam question is likely to give you space to write your own enquiry question so make sure you can remember it.

2 Data collection and results

Complete the following tables to describe the primary data collection techniques and secondary sources that you used. For each technique, summarise the results you found.

Primary techniques	Results
1	
2	
3	
4	

> Remember that primary data (e.g. measurements of longshore drift) is what you collected yourself during your fieldwork.

40

Secondary sources	Outcomes of research
1	
2	
3	
4	

> Secondary data (e.g. census data) is information gathered by other people and organisations.

3 Data presentation

List three ways in which you presented your data and state why you chose that style of presentation.

- ....
- ....
- ....

> For this activity, it might be useful to refer back to the types of graph that are included within the specification. These are shown in Chapter 1 on page 10.

4 Analysis and explanation

What does your fieldwork data tell you? Link this to the geographical ideas you studied.

....
....
....

> An example of a geographical idea would be longshore drift, the formation of spits or river management. It is the geographical concept or idea that underpins your fieldwork. You might have been throwing oranges into the sea and measuring the distance they travelled over five minutes to test the geographical idea of longshore drift.

5 Conclusion

Reread your enquiry question. Summarise the conclusion to your question, based on the outcomes of your fieldwork. Refer to your data to support your conclusions.

....
....
....
....
....

6 Evaluation

a) Identify two **limitations** of your fieldwork and suggest how the validity of the data could be improved if you were to carry out the fieldwork again.

- ....
- ....

b) How reliable is your conclusion?

....
....
....

> Limitations refer to the factors that might make your data inaccurate or the problems you encountered while conducting your fieldwork.

Questions on the Resource Booklet unfamiliar fieldwork

Coasts fieldwork

A student is using the data collection table in Figure 2.13 to gather primary data about sea defences in a coastal landscape.

Figure 2.13 Coastal fieldwork data collection table

LOCATION: Langstone Rock							TYPE OF DEFENCE: Sea Wall
Negative evaluation	-3	-2	-1	1	2	3	Positive evaluation
Vulnerable to erosion							Effective protection against erosion
Vulnerable to overtopping							Effective against overtopping
Ugly							Enhances natural environment
Poor access to beach							Good provision made for access to beach
High-risk safety hazard to general public							No obvious safety risk to general public
High maintenance costs							Low maintenance costs
Short lifespan							Good life expectancy
High levels of disturbance caused to local people during construction							Low levels of disturbance caused to local people during construction
Disturbs natural coastal processes & habitats							Maintains natural coastal processes & habitats

1 Name the technique shown above. *1 mark*

2 Explain one limitation of this data collection method. *2 marks*

Rivers fieldwork

Figure 2.14 The width of sediment samples from three locations along a river (in centimetres)

	1	2	3	4	5	6	7	8	9	10
Upper	15.2	18.5	7.5	11.4	13.0	21.0	16.3	15.2	19.6	11.5
Middle	8.1	3.6	11.5	9.9	7.7	5.3	10.5	12.1	8.2	4.9
Lower	1.3	3.2	0.4	2.7	1.5	0.9	0.4	0.7	4.1	0.4

Refer to Chapter 1, page 12 to help you to calculate the following answers.

3 What is the mode of the sediment in the lower course of the river? *1 mark*

4 What is the interquartile range of the sediment in the upper course? *1 mark*

5 What is the range of the sediment size in the middle course? *1 mark*

8-mark questions based on an unfamiliar fieldwork example

Aim

Students wanted to investigate how the depth and velocity of a river changes across a meander.

Method

To measure the river depth, students held a measuring tape across the river and measured the depth using a metre stick at one metre intervals across the river, from the left hand bank.

The students used an orange to measure the velocity of the river. They released the orange at one metre intervals across the river and used a stopwatch to measure the time taken for the orange to travel 10 metres downstream.

Metres from the bank	Left hand bank	1	2	3	4	5	6	7	8	9	10	11	12
Depth in m	0.27	0.28	0.33	0.42	0.68	0.71	0.65	0.72	0.79	0.80	0.82	0.71	0.67
Velocity (m per second)	0.51	0.64	0.66	0.73	1.14	1.22	1.13	1.31	1.37	1.38	1.40	1.10	0.8

Figure 2.15 Depth and velocity change across a meander on a river in the middle course

Using the data in Figure 2.15 and the axis provided, draw a **cross-section** of the river to show how the depths vary across the river.

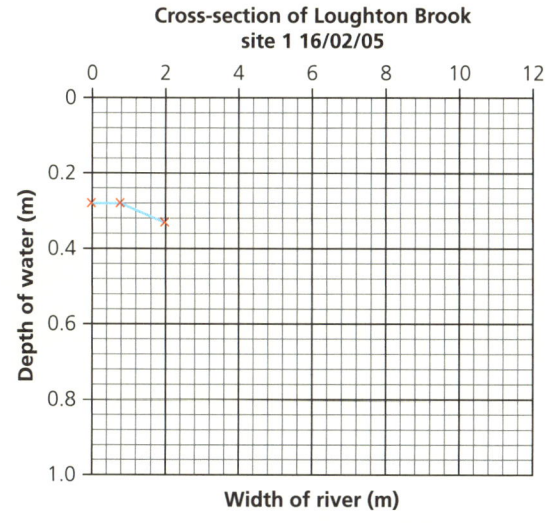

Figure 2.16 Example of a cross-section

Cross-section: a type of line graph used to indicate change in shape and size of a feature. Points should be joined by hand and not using a ruler as they are not straight lines in reality.

6 Using evidence from Figures 2.15 and 2.16, write a conclusion to the hypothesis: 'The depth and velocity of the river are greatest in the middle of the meander.'

8 marks

Can you prove or disprove the hypothesis?

What limitations might there have been in the data collection methods?

How could it have been made more reliable?

8-mark questions based on your fieldwork experience

You will have carried out some physical geography fieldwork as part of your GCSE Geography course.

Enquiry question: ....

To what extent has your fieldwork improved your understanding of the geographical issue?

The geographical issue that was explored during my fieldwork was …

First, the results of the … were …

This … completely/partially/did not help(ed) me to understand the issue because …

Second, the results of the … were …

This … completely/partially/did not help(ed) me to understand the issue because …

Finally, the results of the … were …

This … completely/partially/did not help(ed) me to understand the issue because …

Overall, my fieldwork experience improved my understanding of the issue … *(refer to the Extent-o-meter on page 18)* … because …

Mark scheme

Figure 2.17 A typical mark scheme for the extended fieldwork question

Level 3 (6–8 marks)	Level 2 (3–5 marks)	Level 1 (1–2 marks)
■ **Thorough** analysis and evaluation of how the fieldwork conclusions improved understanding of a geographical issue. ■ **Reasonable** judgement as to whether the fieldwork conclusions improved understanding of a geographical issue. ■ **Well-developed** ideas. ■ There is a well-developed line of reasoning which is clear and **logically structured**. The information presented is relevant and **substantiated**.	■ **Reasonable** analysis and evaluation of how the fieldwork conclusions improved understanding of a geographical issue. ■ **Basic** judgement as to whether the fieldwork conclusions improved understanding of a geographical issue. ■ **Developed** ideas. ■ There is a line of reasoning presented with **some structure**. The information presented is for the most part relevant and **supported by some evidence**.	■ **Basic** analysis and evaluation of how the fieldwork conclusions improved understanding of a geographical question or issue. ■ There will be **no judgement** as to whether the fieldwork conclusions improved understanding of a question or issue. ■ This will be shown by including **simple ideas**. The answer may not link your own fieldwork to a geographical issue. ■ The information is basic and communicated in an **unstructured way**. The information is supported by **limited evidence** and the relationship to the evidence may not be clear.

Important things for you to consider from the mark scheme in Figure 2.17 are:
■ You must make sure that you support your points with evidence from your data, e.g. *Our data revealed that longshore drift was occurring on the day we visited as there were three measurements over five minutes, in which the orange was transported a mean distance of 14.3 metres.*
■ You have to show that you can be evaluative and critical about your fieldwork, e.g. *However, we only recorded the data three times and only on one day, which means that it might not be very reliable as the weather conditions could be very different the next day.*

Spelling, punctuation and grammar

In Paper 1 and Paper 2, the only time you are marked on your spelling, punctuation and grammar (SPaG) is in the final fieldwork question. This makes it a total of 11 marks available (8 marks for the answer and 3 marks available for SPaG). As you can see from the mark scheme in Figure 2.18, your use of key words, or specialist terminology, is very important. But how can you show this off in the fieldwork question? Look in the blue box to the right for some tips.

Figure 2.18 SPaG mark scheme

High performance (3 marks)	You spell and punctuate with **consistent** accuracy. You use rules of grammar with **effective control** of meaning. You use a **wide** range of specialist terms.
Intermediate performance (2 marks)	You spell and punctuate with **considerable** accuracy. You use rules of grammar with **general control** of meaning. You use a **good** range of specialist terms.
Threshold performance (1 mark)	You spell and punctuate with **reasonable** accuracy. You use rules of grammar with **some control** of meaning and any errors do not affect understanding. You use a **limited** range of specialist terms.
0 marks	You have **not written anything**. Your response **does not relate to the question**. Errors **severely impact the meaning** of your answer.

■ Use the geographical words you know from the topic your fieldwork is based on, e.g. if you are assessing coastal management strategies, you might use the following terms: sea walls, rip rap, coastal nourishment, cost-benefit analysis.
■ Use the statistical words you know for analysing data, e.g. range, mean, median.
■ If the question is appropriate, refer to the cartographic and graphical techniques shown on pages 6–7 and 10 in Chapter 1.
■ Other great words to include might be: qualitative (results you have gained from people's opinions) and quantitative (results you have gained that include numbers/data) as well as references to both primary and secondary data.

Chapter 3 Preparing for Paper 2: People and Society

This exam paper contains all of the human geography questions and covers four topics, in the following order:
- Urban Futures
- Dynamic Development
- UK in the 21st century
- Resource Reliance

On pages 47–73 you will practise some of the questions for Paper 2. There is a variety of question styles, ranging from 1-mark 'define' or 'calculate' questions through to more challenging 6- and 8-mark 'assess' and 'evaluate' questions. Use the exam advice and activities to support you through the questions.

As for Paper 1, it is important to remind yourself of the case studies you would expect to see coming up in each topic for the longer-response questions for Paper 2. You are likely to be going into the exam wondering which case studies will appear, as well as having your AO1 knowledge facts stored in your memory!

Use of case studies

Remember that most questions asking you to use your knowledge of case studies will be indicated by the words **CASE STUDY** in capital letters and bold print to help you to spot them easily. Most importantly, you need to identify **which** case study is needed for each of these questions.

> A common mistake for students in Paper 2 is to mix up cities and countries. Urban Futures case studies are CITIES and the Dynamic Development case study is a COUNTRY. As an example, you might be writing about Dhaka in Urban Futures and Zambia in Dynamic Development.

1. Complete the table on page 48 with the case studies that you have been taught as part of your GCSE Geography course for Paper 2 and give three place-specific facts about each case study.

2. Read the following 6-mark questions and write next to them which case study you think you would need to use. Now you have practised the structure of 6-mark questions in Chapter 1, you can try writing the answers to these questions in your notebook.

CASE STUDY – way of life in an AC city

1. For an advanced country (AC) city you have studied, explain how housing and culture contribute to the way of life for people living in the city. **(6 marks)**

CASE STUDY – food security

2. Evaluate the advantages and disadvantages of a present attempt to increase food security. **(8 marks)**

CASE STUDY – UK's political role in a conflict

3. Assess the success of the UK's political role in one global conflict. **(6 marks)**

Topic	Case study required	Your case study	Three place-specific facts
Urban futures	LIDC or EDC city		1 2 3
	AC city		1 2 3
Dynamic development	Low-income developing country (including a top-down and bottom-up development)		1 2 3
UK in the 21st century	Changes in an economic hub		1 2 3
	UK's role in a global conflict		1 2 3
	Contribution of ethnic groups to cultural life of the UK		1 2 3
Resource reliance Attempts to achieve food security in ONE country	An attempt to achieve food security at a **local** scale		1 2 3
	One **past** attempt to achieve food security on a national scale		1 2 3
	One **present** attempt to achieve food security at a national scale		1 2 3

Topic 5: Urban Futures

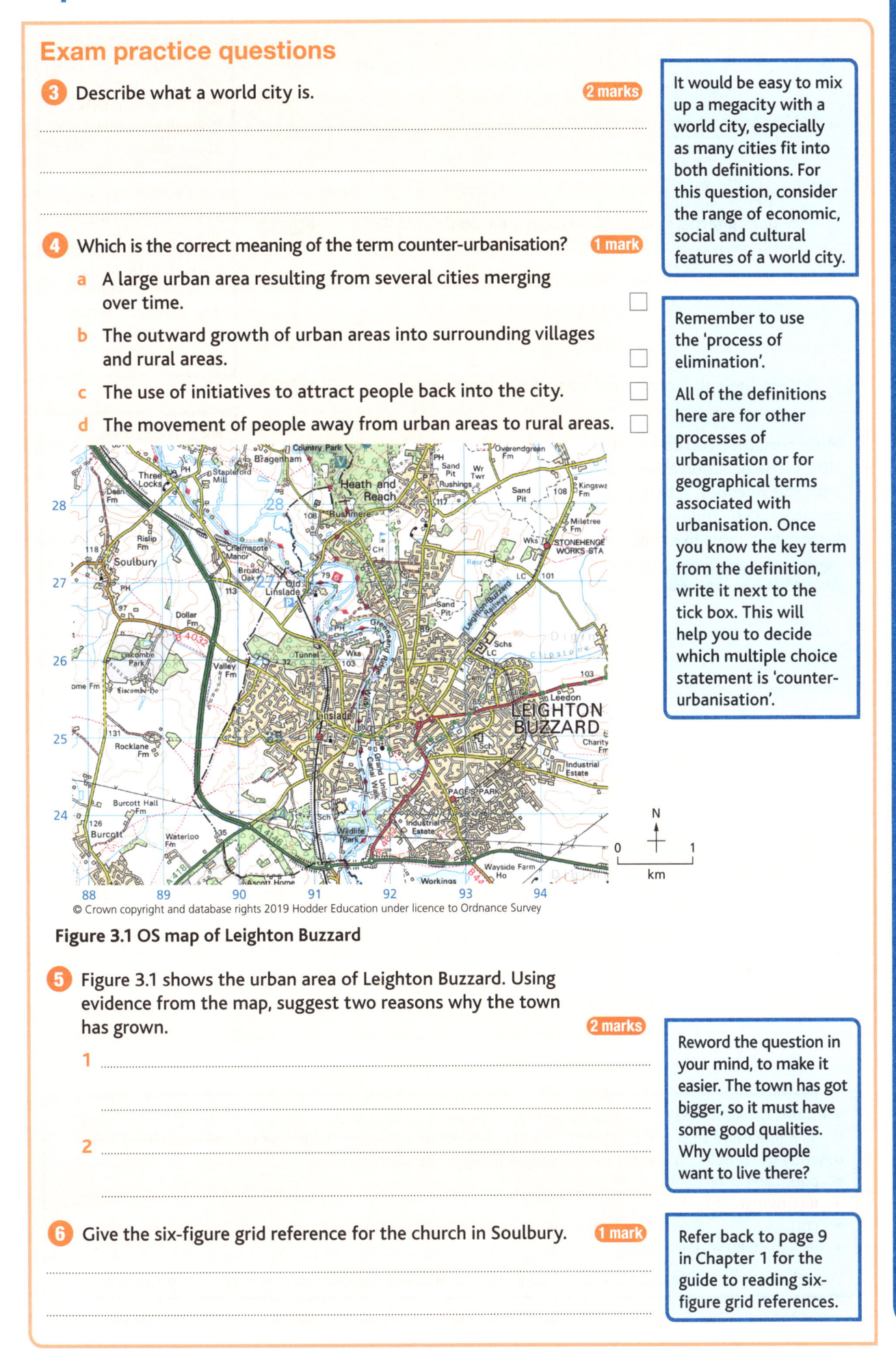

Exam practice questions

3 Describe what a world city. **2 marks**

....

....

....

> It would be easy to mix up a megacity with a world city, especially as many cities fit into both definitions. For this question, consider the range of economic, social and cultural features of a world city.

4 Which is the correct meaning of the term counter-urbanisation? **1 mark**

  a A large urban area resulting from several cities merging over time. ☐

  b The outward growth of urban areas into surrounding villages and rural areas. ☐

  c The use of initiatives to attract people back into the city. ☐

  d The movement of people away from urban areas to rural areas. ☐

> Remember to use the 'process of elimination'.
>
> All of the definitions here are for other processes of urbanisation or for geographical terms associated with urbanisation. Once you know the key term from the definition, write it next to the tick box. This will help you to decide which multiple choice statement is 'counter-urbanisation'.

Figure 3.1 OS map of Leighton Buzzard

© Crown copyright and database rights 2019 Hodder Education under licence to Ordnance Survey

5 Figure 3.1 shows the urban area of Leighton Buzzard. Using evidence from the map, suggest two reasons why the town has grown. **2 marks**

  1 ....

  ....

  2 ....

  ....

> Reword the question in your mind, to make it easier. The town has got bigger, so it must have some good qualities. Why would people want to live there?

6 Give the six-figure grid reference for the church in Soulbury. **1 mark**

....

....

> Refer back to page 9 in Chapter 1 for the guide to reading six-figure grid references.

7 State two consequences of counter-urbanisation. **2 marks**

1 ....

2 ....

> Students often confuse the processes that happen in ACs with the processes that happen in LIDCs. If you have a question about suburbanisation, counter-urbanisation and re-urbanisation, you are focusing your thoughts in ACs.
>
> If the question asks about rural–urban migration or internal growth, you are focusing on LIDCs.

8 Why does internal growth cause rapid urbanisation in LIDCs? **3 marks**

....

9 Explain the pull factors into urban areas in LIDCs. **4 marks**

> Make sure that you do not simply list the pull factors into the city in LIDCs. The question asked you to 'explain' them. The greatest danger with this question is that you would include push factors from the countryside by mistake. To help you to avoid this, add the push and pull factors to a table like this:
>
> | Push factors (out of the countryside) | Pull factors (into the cities) |
> |---|---|
> | | |

> For this question, there are two key factors involved in internal growth. Internal growth occurs when the birth rates are greater than the death rates within the city. Think carefully about what might have led to birth rates increasing and death rates decreasing.
>
> As this is an 'explain' question, make sure that at least one of your points is developed with a '...which means that...' connective.

10 Describe **one** challenge faced by people living in squatter settlements. **3 marks**

....

> With this question you should aim to develop your point as fully as possible. You will not gain more marks if you name more than one challenge. Consider any of the following challenges (or your own idea) and describe the problem it creates for the people living in the slum:
> - poor sanitation
> - unemployment
> - crime
> - lack of clean water.
>
> You will need to practise using '... which means that ...' and '... as a result of this ...' to keep extending the point.

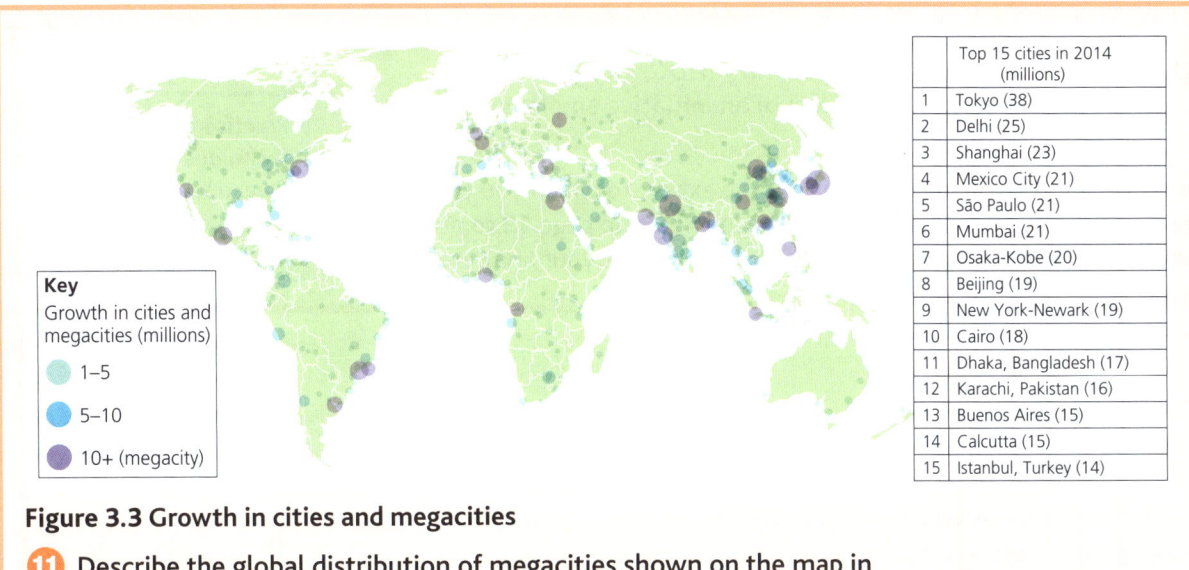

	Top 15 cities in 2014 (millions)
1	Tokyo (38)
2	Delhi (25)
3	Shanghai (23)
4	Mexico City (21)
5	São Paulo (21)
6	Mumbai (21)
7	Osaka-Kobe (20)
8	Beijing (19)
9	New York-Newark (19)
10	Cairo (18)
11	Dhaka, Bangladesh (17)
12	Karachi, Pakistan (16)
13	Buenos Aires (15)
14	Calcutta (15)
15	Istanbul, Turkey (14)

Key
Growth in cities and megacities (millions)
- 1–5
- 5–10
- 10+ (megacity)

Figure 3.3 Growth in cities and megacities

11 Describe the global distribution of megacities shown on the map in Figure 3.3. **3 marks**

> **12** Use CLOCC to annotate the map with the key points you notice about the global distribution.

> Now use TEA to write your answer, making sure you refer to specific countries and continents.

13 For an advanced country (AC) city you have studied, assess the challenges that affect life in the city. **6 marks** ⏱ 7

> **14** For as many challenges as you have studied (e.g. pressure on transport networks, inequality), decide which you think are the greatest to the smallest challenges for the city you studied. Write your place-specific knowledge in the correct place along the continuum below.
>
> Smallest challenge ●────────────────────────● Greatest challenge
>
> In your notebook, write the answer to the question above and then answer the same question but for your LIDC city case study.

Chapter 3 Preparing for Paper 2: People and Society

15 For a low-income developing country (LIDC) city you have studied, assess the success of an initiative employed to make it more sustainable. **6 marks**

Practise the BUG technique on Question 15. Use page 4 to remind yourself how to do this.

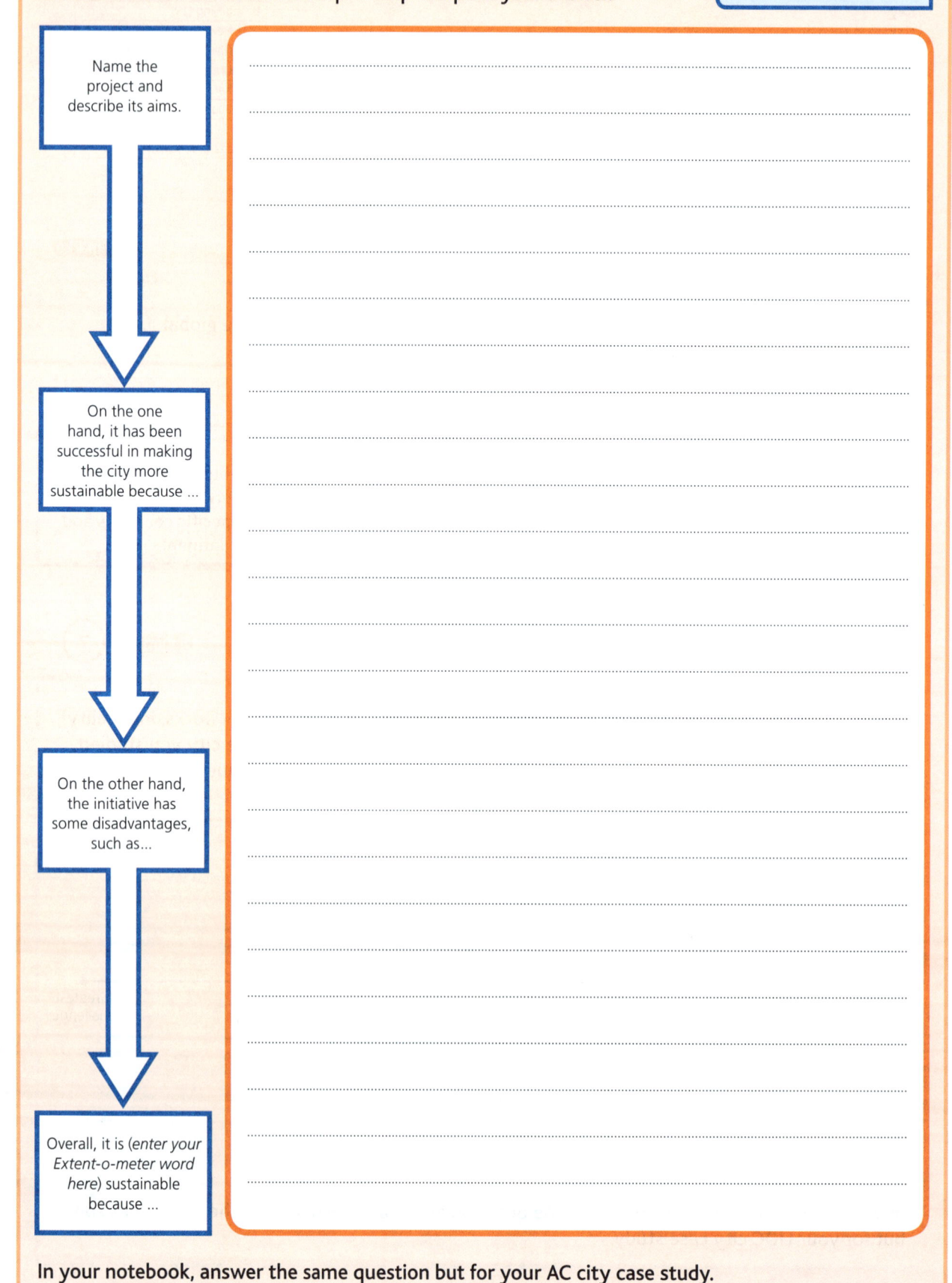

For this question, you need to consider the extent to which you think it has been successful. Refer back to the Extent-o-meter on page 18 to help you decide. Then use the structure strip to help complete your answer.

Name the project and describe its aims.

On the one hand, it has been successful in making the city more sustainable because …

On the other hand, the initiative has some disadvantages, such as…

Overall, it is (*enter your Extent-o-meter word here*) sustainable because …

In your notebook, answer the same question but for your AC city case study.

Topic 6: Dynamic Development

Exam practice questions

16 Which development indicators are used to create the Human Development Index (HDI?) **1 mark**

   a Literacy rate, doctors per 1000 people and life expectancy ☐

   b GDP per capita, education and life expectancy ☐

   c Birth rate, death rate and life expectancy ☐

   d Infant mortality rate, life expectancy and GDP per capita ☐

> Use the 'process of elimination' to remove the answers you know to be incorrect.

17 Using Figure 3.4, describe the global distribution of LIDCs. **3 marks**

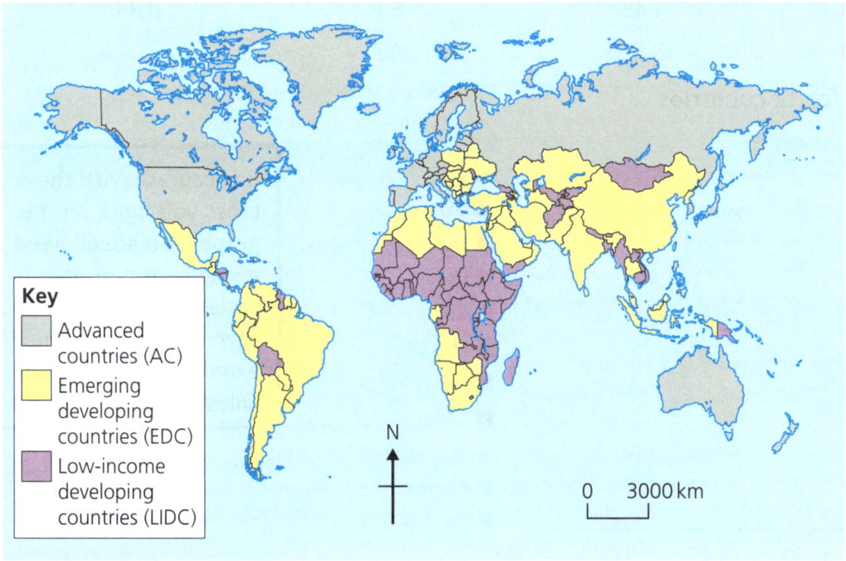

Figure 3.4 IMF country classifications

> You are not required to use data, so the TEA technique would be most useful:
>
> **Trend** (general pattern)
>
> **Example** (name countries)
>
> **Anomaly**
>
> Use the name of continents and countries to add detail to your answer and show your abilities as a geographer!

53

Country	Life expectancy	GNI per capita $	Infant mortality rate	Literacy rate %
UK	80.9	40,530	4.2	99.0
USA	80.1	58,270	5.7	99.0
France	82.0	37,970	3.2	99.0
Brazil	74.3	8,600	16.9	92.6
China	75.8	8,690	11.8	96.4
India	69.1	1,800	37.8	71.2
Ethiopia	63.0	740	48.3	49.1
South Africa	64.1	5,430	29.9	94.4
Chile	79.1	13,610	6.4	97.5
Indonesia	73.2	3,540	21.9	95.4
Kuwait	78.3	31,430	6.8	95.7
Mexico	76.3	8,610	11.3	94.5

Figure 3.5 Development data for 12 countries

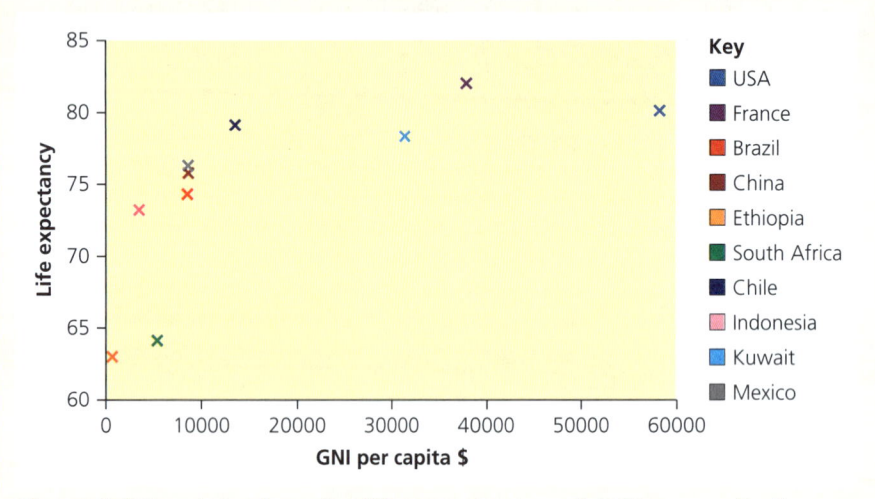

Figure 3.6 Graph to show the life expectancy and GDP per capita for 12 countries

18 Using the data for life expectancy and GDP per capita in Figure 3.5, plot the locations for the UK and India on the scatter graph in Figure 3.6. **2 marks**

19 Draw a line of best fit on the graph. **1 mark**

20 Calculate the mean infant mortality rate. **1 mark**

Be accurate with the cross you mark on the graph. You are allowed a small amount of variation on the correct answer in the exam, but accuracy will secure the mark.

When adding your line of best fit, ensure that there are the same number of crosses above the line as there are below it.

21 Calculate the mode of the literacy rate. **1 mark**

Remember that mode is the most common value.

22 Calculate the interquartile range of the life expectancy data. Show your workings. **2 marks**

Refer back to page 12 in Chapter 1 to remind yourself how to calculate the interquartile range.

23 Explain how **debt** can make it hard for countries to break out of poverty. [4 marks]

Here is an answer from a GCSE student showing the 'so what?' moments. This is an excellent example of how to take one idea and continue to extend and develop the point.

> Debt makes it incredibly difficult for countries to break out of poverty,

SO WHAT?

> because when they get given money from other countries, they are made to pay all the money back with interest.

SO WHAT?

> This means that they have less money to spend on services such as education systems and healthcare.

SO WHAT?

> This sets the country back even further because if you don't have a good education system then no one can get better jobs and if everyone is too sick to get jobs, the country does not make any money.

> This is a great opportunity to show you the importance of asking 'so what?' When you write one idea, continue to develop it by thinking 'so what?' until you cannot develop the idea any further.

24 Explain how **trade** can make it hard for countries to break out of poverty. [4 marks]

> Now use the student's answer from Question 23 to help you write your own answer to Question 24.

25 Explain two physical factors that influence uneven development. [4 marks]

> Use the PEPE structure to help you write your answer:
>
> | | |
> |---|---|
> | Point | One physical factor is … |
> | Explain | … which influences development by … |
> | Point | A second physical factor is … |
> | Explain | … which influences development by … |

CASE STUDY – Low-income developing country (LIDC)

8 Explain your chosen country's stage on the Rostow Model. **(4 marks)**

Use the writing frame to help you structure your answer.

The country of .... is most likely at stage .... because ....

....

....

9 For an LIDC you have studied, assess the advantages and disadvantages of top-down development strategy in the country. **(9) (8 marks)**

Before you try to answer the question, let's pick it apart a little more.

a Name the development strategy.

....

b Why is it an example of top-down development?

....

....

....

Imagine these sorts of questions like a tug-of-war. There are two sides of the argument – the advantages and the disadvantages – but who wins?

Complete the table in your notebook

Advantages	Disadvantages

Because the command word is 'assess', you are going to have to decide whether the advantages win or the disadvantages. Complete the table and use it to write your answer.

This is a good time to remind you that the examiners say you are more likely to gain marks for fewer points that are fully developed than for a series of undeveloped points.

Do not introduce a new point in your concluding comment. Use the points you have already made to reach a substantiated (backed-up) answer to the overall question. Use the following writing frame to help you.

In .... [name the country], a top-down development strategy is

....

An advantage of the strategy is that ....

....

....

56

which means that

As a result of this,

Another advantage is

which means that

As a result of this,

A disadvantage of the strategy is that

which means that

As a result of this,

Another disadvantage is,

which means that

As a result of this,

Overall, the advantages/disadvantages are greater because

Topic 7: The UK in the Twenty-first Century

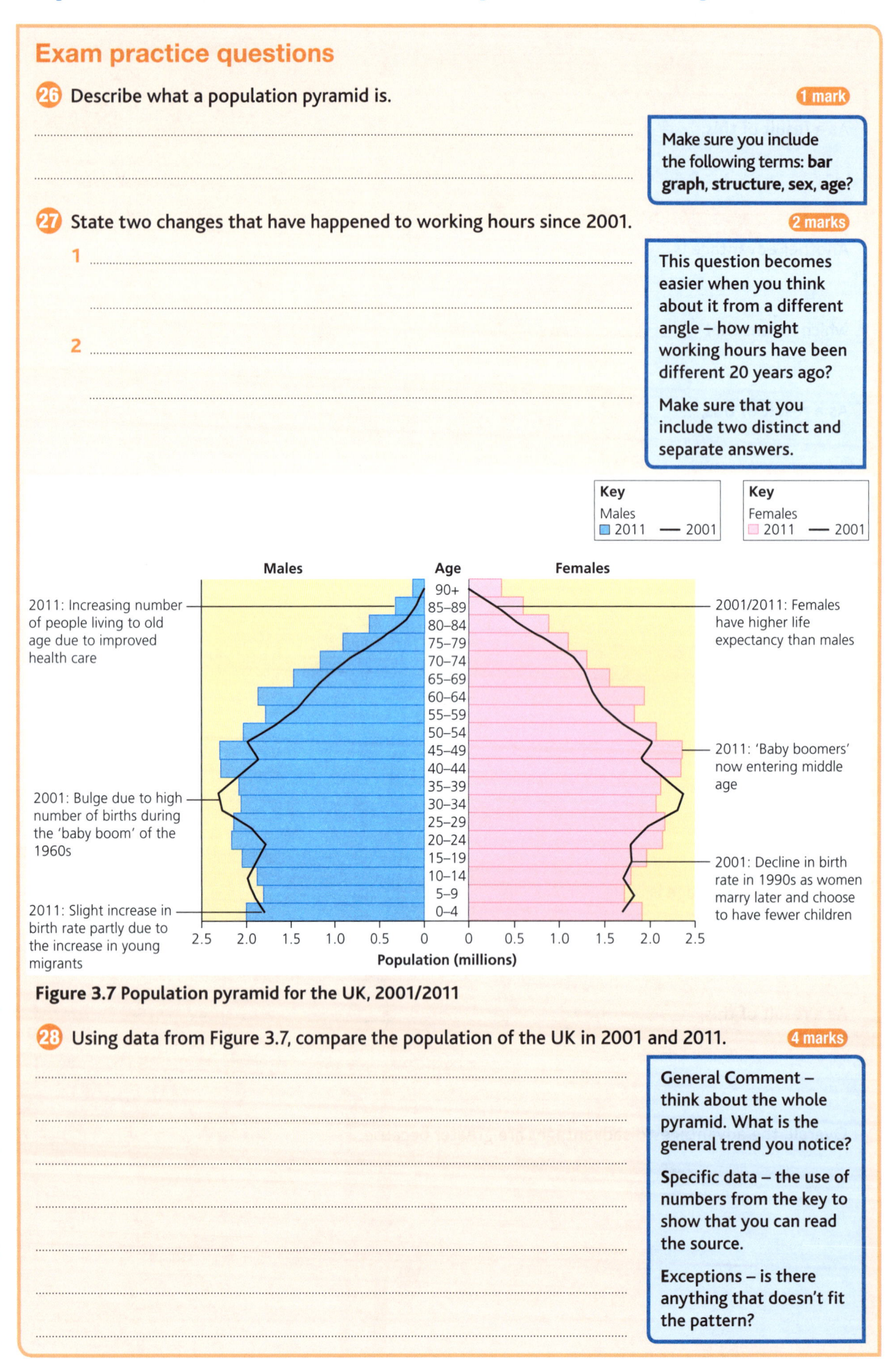

Exam practice questions

26 Describe what a population pyramid is. *(1 mark)*

....

....

> Make sure you include the following terms: **bar graph, structure, sex, age**?

27 State two changes that have happened to working hours since 2001. *(2 marks)*

1 ....

....

2 ....

....

> This question becomes easier when you think about it from a different angle – how might working hours have been different 20 years ago?
>
> Make sure that you include two distinct and separate answers.

Key
Males ■ 2011 — 2001

Key
Females ■ 2011 — 2001

2011: Increasing number of people living to old age due to improved health care

2001/2011: Females have higher life expectancy than males

2011: 'Baby boomers' now entering middle age

2001: Bulge due to high number of births during the 'baby boom' of the 1960s

2001: Decline in birth rate in 1990s as women marry later and choose to have fewer children

2011: Slight increase in birth rate partly due to the increase in young migrants

Figure 3.7 Population pyramid for the UK, 2001/2011

28 Using data from Figure 3.7, compare the population of the UK in 2001 and 2011. *(4 marks)*

....

....

....

....

....

....

....

> **General Comment** – think about the whole pyramid. What is the general trend you notice?
>
> **Specific data** – the use of numbers from the key to show that you can read the source.
>
> **Exceptions** – is there anything that doesn't fit the pattern?

29 Describe the causes of an ageing population in the UK. **3 marks**

....
....
....
....
....

> For this question, the command word is 'describe', not 'state'. Take one point and describe how it leads to people living for longer. There needs to be more detail than you would give for a 'suggest' question.

30 Explain how ethnic groups have made a positive contribution to the cultural life of the UK. **4 marks**

Highlight the elements of PEEL that you can find within this model answer:

In the UK, we eat many foods that originated from other places in the world, including curry from Asia. There are many restaurants that produce authentic ethnic food, which are popular both with people from that ethnic background as well as white British people. An example of this can be found on London Road in Sheffield, which has a large Asian population, with shops selling Indian and Chinese produce. Furthermore, the positive contribution made by ethnic groups is shown through the 'world food' aisles that are found in larger supermarkets.

Now, write your own answer, either using food, media or fashion (depending on which aspect of cultural life you have studied). Refer back to your case study table on page 48 to help you to answer the question.

....
....
....
....
....
....
....

31 Suggest why UK television programmes are a successful media export. **3 marks**

....
....
....
....
....

City	Population density (per sq mile)
London (Inner)	23,410
London (Outer)	8,787
Birmingham	9,725
Leeds	3,365
Liverpool	10,863
Manchester	9,266
Newcastle	6,504
Sheffield	3,720

Figure 3.10 Population density for a variety of UK cities

31 Calculate the range of the population densities. *1 mark*

32 Calculate the median of the population densities. *1 mark*

33 Which of the following would be the most suitable cartographical technique for presenting population densities in the UK? *1 mark*

　a　Choropleth map ☐
　b　Isoline map ☐
　c　Flow line map ☐
　d　Sphere of influence map ☐

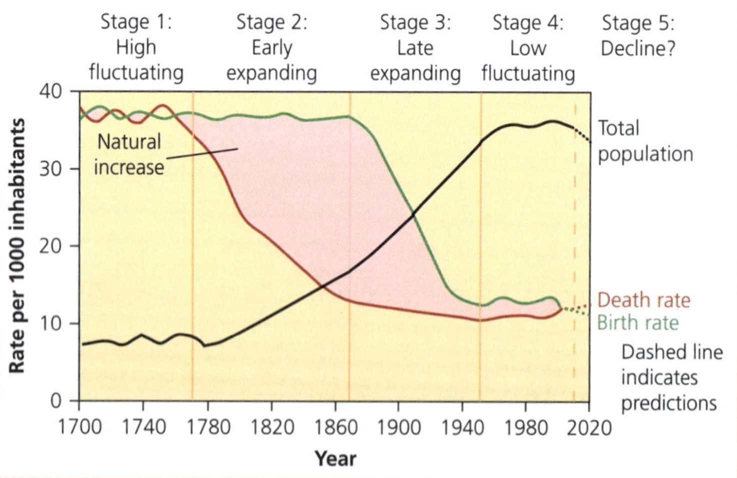

Figure 3.11 The UK demographic transition model

34 Using Figure 3.11, suggest and explain the UK's stage on the demographic transition model. *3 marks*

Use this space for your workings.

Refer back to pages 6–7 in Chapter 1 to remind yourself of the different types of maps.

It may be useful to refer back to Figure 3.7 showing the population pyramid of the UK to help you with answering question 34.

You would get 1 mark for correctly identifying which stage the UK is at on the demographic transition model. Two further marks will come from your explanation of your decision. Consider the birth rate and the death rate.

CASE STUDY: an economic hub in the UK

10 Evaluate the significance of one economic hub within its region and within the rest of the UK.

8 marks

⏱ 9

Annotate the meters with your place specific information

Significance within its region

Not significant — Very significant

Significance in the rest of the UK

Not significant — Very significant

In your answer to question 10 above:
- write one paragraph about the significance of the economic hub within its region
- write one paragraph about the significance of the economic hub within the rest of the UK.

Refer back to the Extent-o-meter (page 18) to decide to what extent you think the economic hub has a greater regional or national significance.

Topic 8: Resource Reliance

Exam practice questions

35 Define the term food security. *1 mark*

....

....

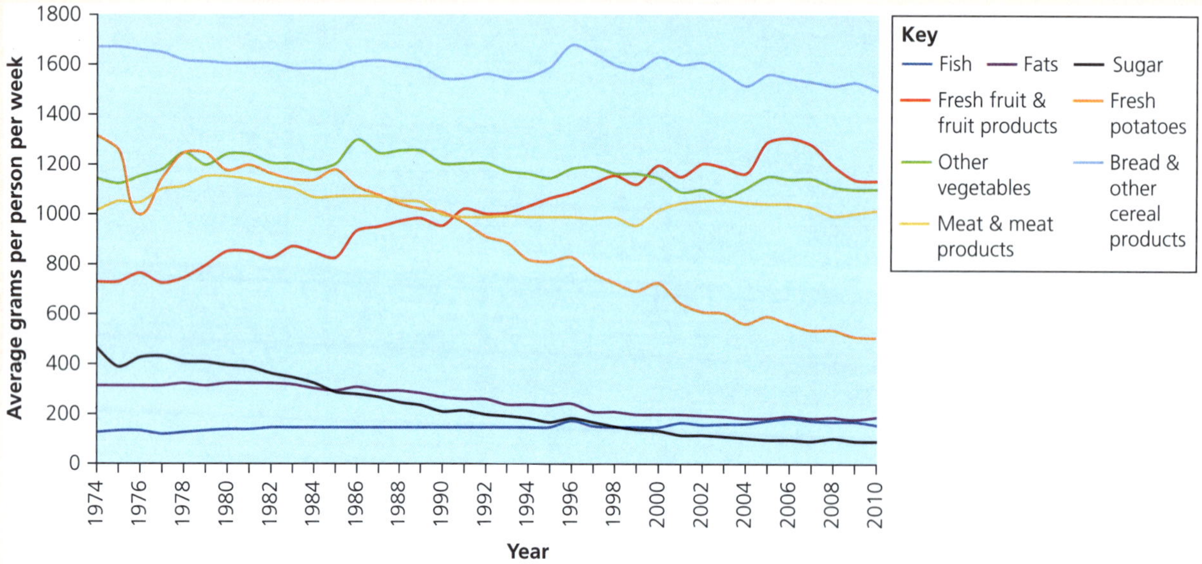

Figure 3.12 Household food consumption in the UK, 1974–2010

36 Using the data in Figure 3.12, describe the pattern of food consumption in the UK. *3 marks*

Some of the information in the student answer below is incorrect. Correct the errors you can find.

> Easy marks can be missed by not reading graphs accurately. Ensure that you use the axis and do not guess the reading or round up.

Student answer

Bread and cereal products are consumed the least and sugar and fish are consumed the most.

The largest decrease over time has been fresh potatoes, which have changed from an average of 1500 grams per person per week in 1974 to only 500 grams per person per week in 2010. Fresh fruit has increased from 750 grams in 1978 to a peak of 1300 in 2006 but has since declined.

Sugar has increased from 875 grams to only 100 grams.

37 Explain what Malthus' theory suggests about the relationship between population and food supply. *4 marks*

Student answer

Thomas Malthus wrote his theory in 1798 and he suggested that population increases geometrically whereas food supply only increases arithmetically. This means that there comes a point when food supply exceeds the population. As a result of this, he proposed there would be a catastrophe involving famine and war. However, he was writing well before modern technology where land becomes more productive and contraception helps to manage the population.

62

38 Explain what Boserup's theory suggests about the relationship between population and food supply. **4 marks**

....
....
....
....
....
....
....
....

> Use the answer to Question 37 about Malthus' theory as a model. Try to use a similar structure to answer the same question but for Boserup's theory. Notice how the model answer includes the use of 'this means that' and 'as a result of this' to keep building on the response.

CASE STUDY – Food security

12 For a country you have studied, explain how food security is achieved by one method at a national scale. **6 marks**

....
....
....
....
....
....
....
....
....
....
....
....
....
....

> First, BUG the question.
>
> The named country can be an AC, EDC or LIDC. You can only get a maximum of Level 1 if you talk about the incorrect scale example.
>
> Your answer must also be place-specific. This is usually demonstrated through your AO1 facts about your case study/ example.
>
> A top Level 3 answer will show thorough knowledge of one national scale method to improve food security (AO1) with thorough understanding of how food security has been achieved through this method (AO2).
>
> Well-developed ideas are needed, so consider the 'so what?' idea throughout your answer. How many times can you keep extending your ideas?

| 29% | 31% | 5% | 2% | 4% | |

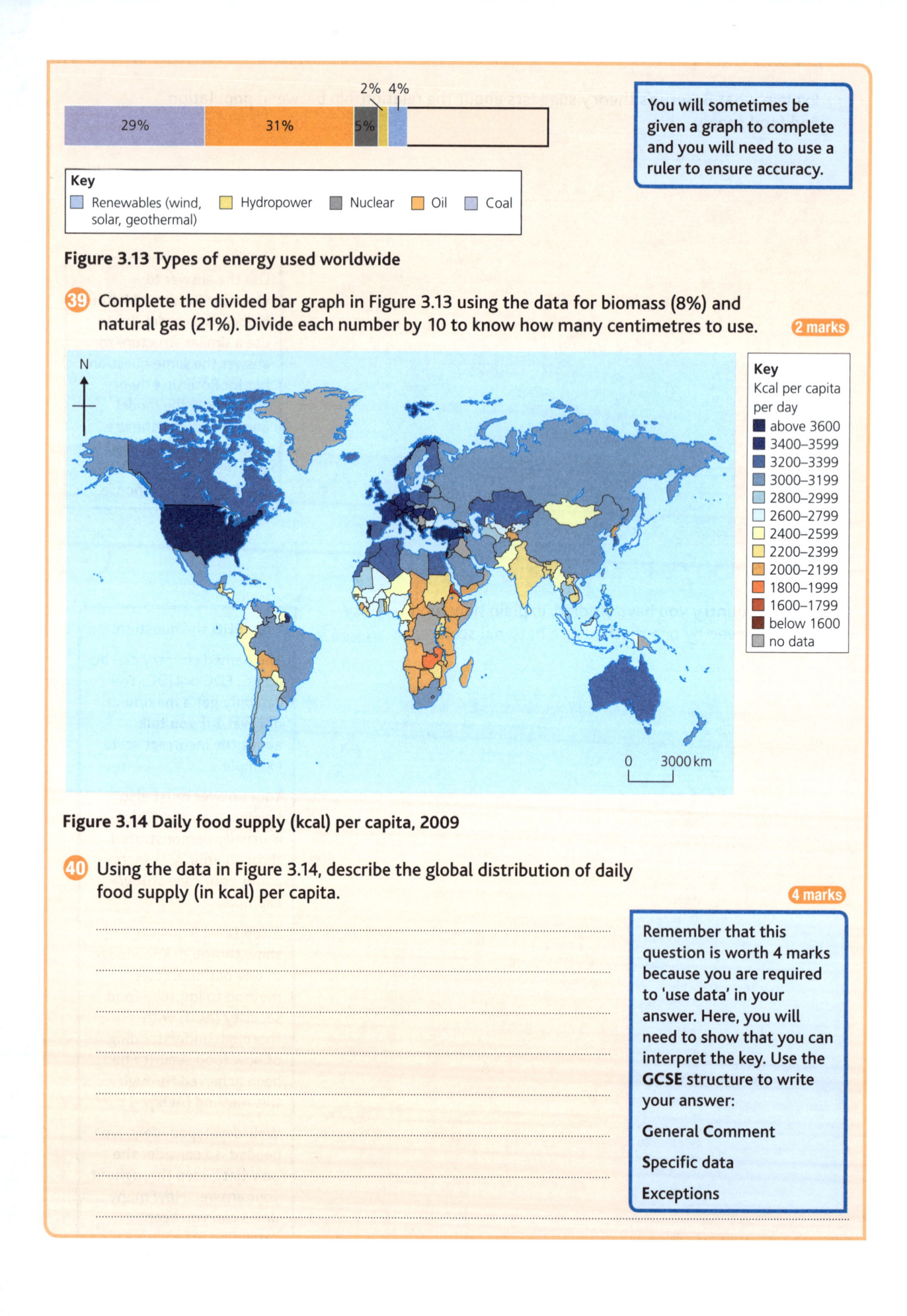

Key
- Renewables (wind, solar, geothermal)
- Hydropower
- Nuclear
- Oil
- Coal

Figure 3.13 Types of energy used worldwide

> You will sometimes be given a graph to complete and you will need to use a ruler to ensure accuracy.

39 Complete the divided bar graph in Figure 3.13 using the data for biomass (8%) and natural gas (21%). Divide each number by 10 to know how many centimetres to use. **2 marks**

Figure 3.14 Daily food supply (kcal) per capita, 2009

Key — Kcal per capita per day:
- above 3600
- 3400–3599
- 3200–3399
- 3000–3199
- 2800–2999
- 2600–2799
- 2400–2599
- 2200–2399
- 2000–2199
- 1800–1999
- 1600–1799
- below 1600
- no data

40 Using the data in Figure 3.14, describe the global distribution of daily food supply (in kcal) per capita. **4 marks**

> Remember that this question is worth 4 marks because you are required to 'use data' in your answer. Here, you will need to show that you can interpret the key. Use the **GCSE** structure to write your answer:
>
> **General Comment**
>
> **Specific data**
>
> **Exceptions**

41 Suggest two reasons for the global distribution of daily food supply. **2 marks**

1 ....

2 ....

42 Explain why the demand for water in some parts of the world outstrips supply. **3 marks**

....
....
....
....

43 Explain how the mechanisation of farming can affect ecosystems. **3 marks**

....
....
....

> You can access the marks with three single ideas, but you would also get credit for any developed points.

....
....

44 <u>Evaluate</u> whether <u>physical</u> or <u>human factors</u> have a greater effect on <u>food security</u>. **8 marks**

45 You might also be given a 6- or 8-mark question that does not directly involve a case study. List the physical and human factors affecting food security below. Aim to include at least three in each column.

Physical	Human

46 Rank all the points in your table in order from the factor you consider to have the greatest effect on food security to the smallest. This will help you to tackle the **AO3 evaluate** element of the question.

47 Write your answer to question 44 on page 66, using the prompts in the structure strip on page 66 to help you. When choosing the three factors to use from your table, select them from across the range of your rankings to make it easier to reach a judgement.

Chapter 3 Preparing for Paper 2: People and Society

Write a **simple definition** of food security.

Write a well-developed point about the first factor.

Write a well-developed point about a second factor.

Write a well-developed point about a third factor.

Write a concluding paragraph – which factor has the most/least effect on food security and why?

Section B: Human geography fieldwork

In this section you will be asked similar questions to the ones in Paper 1. You will be asked a selection of AO4 (skills) questions that might ask you to:
- use statistics to analyse your fieldwork data
- suggest appropriate ways to present data
- state primary and secondary methods of data collection.

You will also be given an 8-mark question either about the fieldwork you carried out or about fieldwork results contained in the Resource Booklet. In either case you will be asked to explore any area of the enquiry process, such as:
- Discuss and evaluate fieldwork techniques
- Reach a conclusion to the fieldwork.

This chapter gives you the opportunity to practise both questions on your own fieldwork and on fieldwork that has already been completed.

> You should have completed a fieldwork experience in a human environment (e.g. in a city centre, village, new out-of-town shopping centre). To help you to organise your fieldwork notes, complete the questions over these two pages. The activities take you sequentially through the fieldwork process, from deciding on your question to reaching a conclusion.

My fieldwork record

1 Route to enquiry

a Location and date of fieldwork:

Shrewsbury   May 17th 2022

b Enquiry question:

To what extend does big town plan helps you to answer overall question for investigation.

2 Data collection and results

Complete the following table to state the primary data collection techniques and secondary sources that you used. For each technique, summarise the results you found.

Primary techniques	Results
1 interviewing people	
2 Environmental quality	
3 Questionair	
4 my own opinion	

Secondary sources	Outcomes of research
1 Glenn Howells Architects	
2 Council	
3	
4	

> Remember that **primary data (e.g. footfall surveys)** is what you collected yourself during your fieldwork.

> **Secondary data (e.g. census data)** is information gathered by other people and organisations.

3 Data presentation

List three ways in which you presented your data and state why you chose that style of presentation.

1. ....
2. ....
3. ....

> For this activity, it might be useful to refer back to the types of graph that are included within the specification. These are shown in Chapter 1 on page 10.

Analysis and explanation

What does your fieldwork data tell you? Link this to the geographical ideas you have studied.

....
....
....
....
....

Conclusion

Reread your enquiry question. Summarise the conclusion to your question based on the outcomes of your fieldwork. Refer to your data to support your conclusions.

....
....
....
....
....
....
....

Evaluation

a Identify two **limitations** of your fieldwork and suggest how the validity of the data could be improved if you were to carry out the fieldwork again.

- ....
- ....

b How reliable is your conclusion?

....
....
....
....

> **Limitations** refer to the factors that might make your data inaccurate or the problems you encountered while conducting your fieldwork.

Fieldwork practice questions

1. Suggest a secondary data collection technique suitable for carrying out human geography fieldwork. **1 mark**

....

....

2. Complete the bar graph in Figure 3.15. The pedestrian count for Saint Martin's Square was 63.

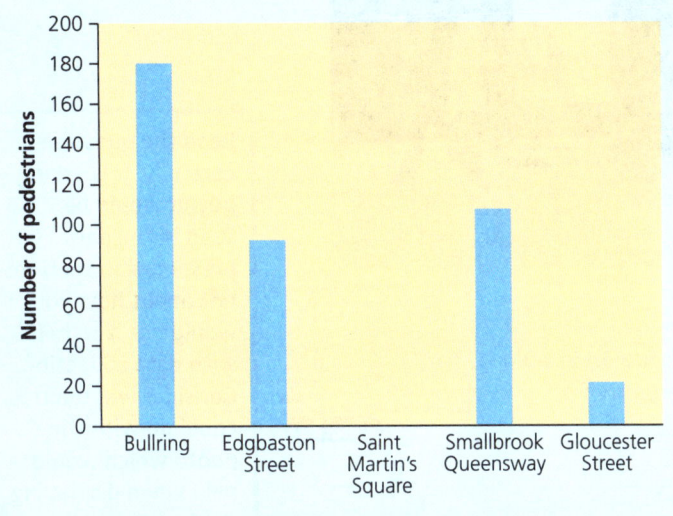

Figure 3.15 Pedestrian counts measured over five minutes in Birmingham city centre

3. Calculate the median pedestrian count. **1 mark**

....

4. Calculate the interquartile range of pedestrian counts. **1 mark**

....

5. For a human geography fieldwork investigation which you have completed, evaluate one technique you used to collect your data. **2 marks**

....

....

....

....

> This question is asking you to evaluate your fieldwork. It is not asking you to describe how you collected the data. Ask yourself what went well when you collected it as well as what problems you encountered. Was the reliability of your data affected?
>
> Make sure you name the technique you used, although the 2 marks are entirely for your evaluation of the technique.

Figure 3.16 New Street in Birmingham

6 State two ways in which the photograph in Figure 3.16 could be used effectively in the data presentation section of a student's fieldwork investigation. **2 marks**

a ....

b ....

> Read the question carefully. It is asking how it would be used in the data presentation section, not about how you would use it to help with data collection. Consider what you could do with the photo which would help when displaying fieldwork data.

Environmental quality scores

Location	Score
Bullring Shopping Centre	+16
Edgbaston Street	+6
Saint Martin's Square	+9
Smallbrook Queensway	−11
Gloucester Street	−5

Figure 3.17 Environmental quality scores for five locations in Birmingham city centre

> To explore these streets in more detail, use Google Maps in satellite view and street view.

Questionnaire responses

People in Birmingham city centre were asked a series of questions as part of a questionnaire. Figure 3.18 shows some of the responses to one of the questions.

Do you think the regeneration of the Bullring shopping centre has had a positive impact on the city centre?

- It has been very positive! It is a well-maintained and popular location and many of the major chain shops are there.
- The iconic bull outside helps to link the modern development to its heritage so that it doesn't just appear the same as any other shopping centre in the country.
- The problem has been the number of shops left empty in other streets when some retailers moved into the indoor shopping mall. These shops have just been left and are making other areas look poor.
- It can get very busy and overcrowded at times, particularly on a Saturday.

Figure 3.18 Questionnaire given to people in Birmingham

Bullring Centre Fact File
- The Bullring indoor shopping centre opened on 4 September 2003.
- It was the busiest in the UK in 2004, with 36.5 million visitors.
- It has one of only four Selfridges department stores in the UK.
- There is 110,000 m² of retail space,
- When it opened, more than 8000 jobs were created within the new Bullring.
- There are over 140 shops and kiosks.

8-mark questions based on an unfamiliar fieldwork example

7 Using evidence from Figures 3.17–3.18 and the fact file above write a conclusion to the hypothesis: 'The regeneration of Birmingham's Bullring shopping centre has been successful.' Develop your answer.

8 marks
SpaG 3 marks

8-mark question based on your fieldwork experience

You will have carried out some human geography fieldwork as part of your GCSE Geography course.

Name the fieldwork: ....

8 To what extent was your primary data collection successful? **8 marks**

Below is an example of how a student has written a PEEL paragraph in response to this question. Focus particularly on the AO3 element in which the student has **evaluated** their primary data collection technique.

Student answer

While investigating the success of urban regeneration in Plymouth, we conducted an environmental quality survey. — **Point**

This involved the scoring of features such as graffiti, presence of green space, attractiveness of building, using a scale of −3 to +3. — **Explanation**

This produced a score for five different zones of the city centre, with Drake's Circus having the highest score of +16. — **Evidence**

This was mostly successful as it enabled me to compare the quality of the environment in each location. However, it was subjective so the scores across the class varied, making it less reliable. — **Link back to the question**

9 Now, for your own fieldwork experience, write your answer in the space below, using the PEEL prompts to help you. You should aim to discuss three primary data collection methods that you used.

Method 1	P
	E
	E
	L
Method 2	P
	E
	E
	L
Method 3	P
	E
	E
	L

Overall, which was the most/least successful?

Mark scheme

Level 3 (6–8 marks)	Level 2 (3–5 marks)	Level 1 (1–2 marks)
Thorough evaluation (AO3) of the primary data collection methods used with a **thorough** judgement as to the extent of their success (AO3). **Well-developed** ideas. **Well-developed** line of reasoning which is **clear and logically structured**. The information presented is **relevant** and **substantiated**.	**Reasonable** evaluation (AO3) of the primary data collection methods used with a **reasonable** judgement as to the extent of their success (AO3). **Developed** ideas. There is a line of reasoning presented with **some structure**. The information presented is **mostly relevant** and supported by **some evidence**.	**Basic** evaluation (AO3) of the primary data collection methods used with a **basic** judgement as to the extent of their success (AO3). **Simple** ideas. The information is **basic** and communicated in an **unstructured way**. The information is supported by **limited** evidence and the **relationship to the evidence may not be clear**.

Figure 3.19 Mark scheme for fieldwork questions

10 Using Figure 3.19, suggest three differences between a Level 3 response to a fieldwork question and a Level 1 response.

11 Read your answer on page 72.

Based on the mark scheme for the question:

a How many marks do you think it would have been given?

b How could you have improved your answer?

Chapter 4 Preparing for Paper 3

In this chapter, you will work through a series of questions related to a topical geographical issue. This paper tests your ability to think and communicate like a geographer and the best candidates will be able to apply their knowledge from across topics to the one issue explored in the paper. This is known as **synopticity**.

Making synoptic links

1. In the space provided between the two topics from Paper 1 and Paper 2, write a statement which explains how they could be linked. To stretch yourself, try to give a place-specific example. The first one has been completed for you.

Topic	Can you make a link between the two topics?	Topic
Global Hazards	Many megacities are also in locations that are vulnerable to tectonic and climatic hazards. For example, Manilla in the Philippines is in the path of tropical storms travelling across the Pacific Ocean.	Urban Futures
Sustaining Ecosystems		Resource Reliance
Changing Climate		UK in the Twenty-first Century
Distinctive Landscapes		Dynamic Development
Sustaining Ecosystems		Urban Futures
Global Hazards		Dynamic Development
Changing Climate		Resource Reliance

How to write like a geographer

The STEEP model shown in Figure 4.1 is a useful tool for helping you to think and write like a geographer. For any geographical issue, you will need to consider the following aspects:

- **S**ocial
- **T**echnological
- **E**conomic
- **E**nvironmental
- **P**olitical.

In the last question of Paper 3, you have to make a geographical decision. This will sometimes be a choice between two options and sometimes you will have to suggest your own idea. In order to evaluate the strengths and weaknesses of any geographical decision, you can use the questions in the STEEP model. It might be the case that not all aspects of the STEEP model are applicable to the issue you are exploring, so be selective. Once you have determined how good the geographical decision would be regarding each of the aspects, you can come to a conclusion. Using the STEEP model will help you not only to reach a good geographical decision but also to explain *why* your decision is a good one.

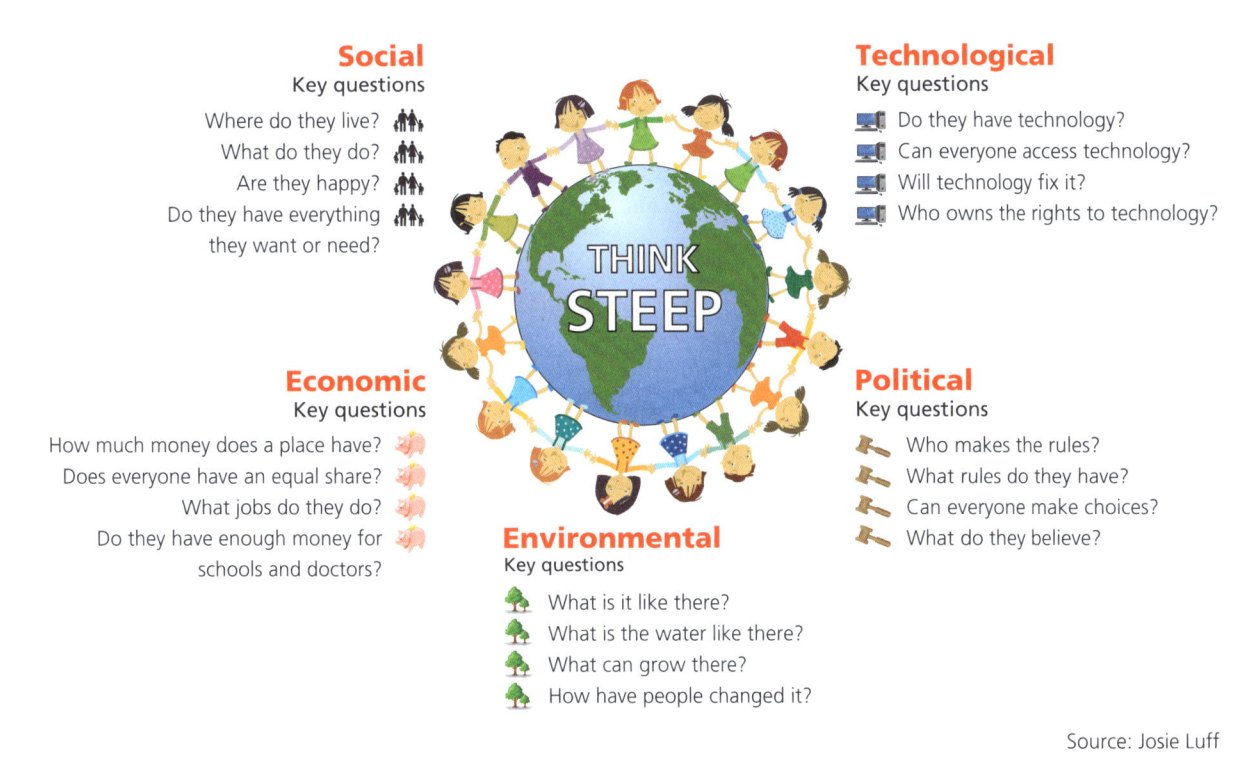

Social
Key questions
- Where do they live?
- What do they do?
- Are they happy?
- Do they have everything they want or need?

Technological
Key questions
- Do they have technology?
- Can everyone access technology?
- Will technology fix it?
- Who owns the rights to technology?

Economic
Key questions
- How much money does a place have?
- Does everyone have an equal share?
- What jobs do they do?
- Do they have enough money for schools and doctors?

Environmental
Key questions
- What is it like there?
- What is the water like there?
- What can grow there?
- How have people changed it?

Political
Key questions
- Who makes the rules?
- What rules do they have?
- Can everyone make choices?
- What do they believe?

Source: Josie Luff

Figure 4.1 The STEEP model

Practice Paper 3: The future of Antarctica

This exam will be accompanied by a detailed Resource Booklet to present you with the geographical issue. The Paper 3 example in this workbook focuses mainly on sustaining ecosystems, while giving you the chance to draw on other topics in your extended writing.

You will need to spend AT LEAST 10 minutes exploring the Resource Booklet and reading all of the questions so that you fully understand the geographical issue. Make sure you read the final question carefully. Your ideas to support this decision will develop as you work through the exam paper.

This chapter includes a mock Resource Booklet comprising a series of exam questions similar to those you would find in the exam. Use the guided help with each of the questions to help you to develop the exam technique needed to tackle the real Paper 3 exam.

Resource Booklet checklist

When exploring the Resource Booklet for the first time, you need to do the following:

- **R**ead the resources carefully.
- **A**nnotate any graphs and photos with their key features – think about TEA!
- Think about the **S**ynoptic links you can make between the resources and the other topics in the course.
- **H**ighlight the key geographical words and annotate with the definitions.

> To remind yourself to complete these four stages in the exam, write 'R, A, S, H' at the top of the Resource Booklet (read, annotate, synoptic links, highlight).

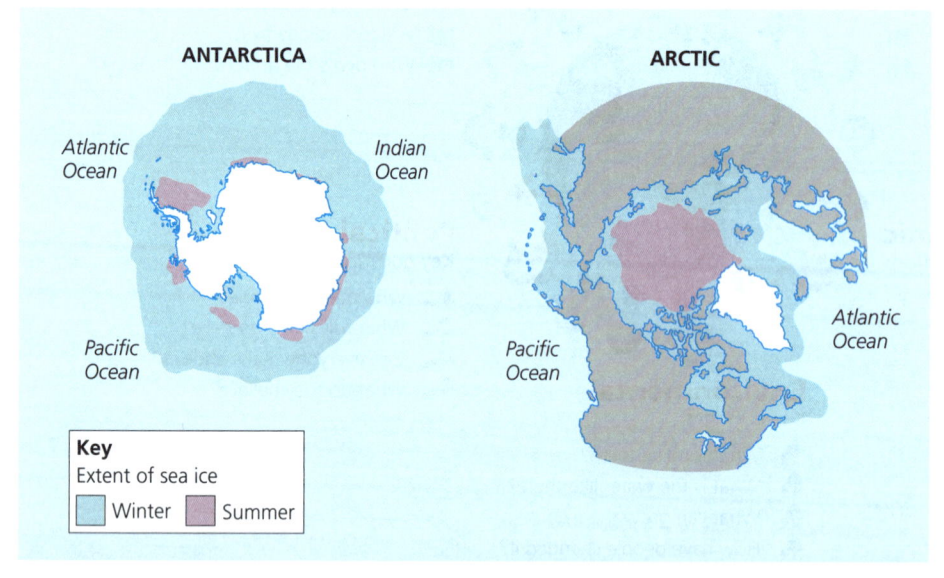

Antarctica	Arctic
• It is covered by an ice sheet 2.8 miles thick in some places.	• It is warmer than Antarctica.
• Winter temperatures vary from −62°C to −55°C.	• Winter temperatures vary from −46°C to −26°C.
• Al the weather is kept within Antarctica due to the circumpolar winds travelling around the coastline.	• The sea does not fall below −2°C as it is influenced by the Gulf Stream and weather systems moving northwards.
• It has an average height of 2300 metres.	• Mosses, grasses and alpine-like shrubs are found.
• Flora is less plentiful.	• Fauna includes reindeer, polar bears and whales.
• Fauna includes penguins, whales and seals.	

Figure 4.2 The polar regions – Antarctica and the Arctic

Figure 4.3 A killer whale hunting seals in Antarctica

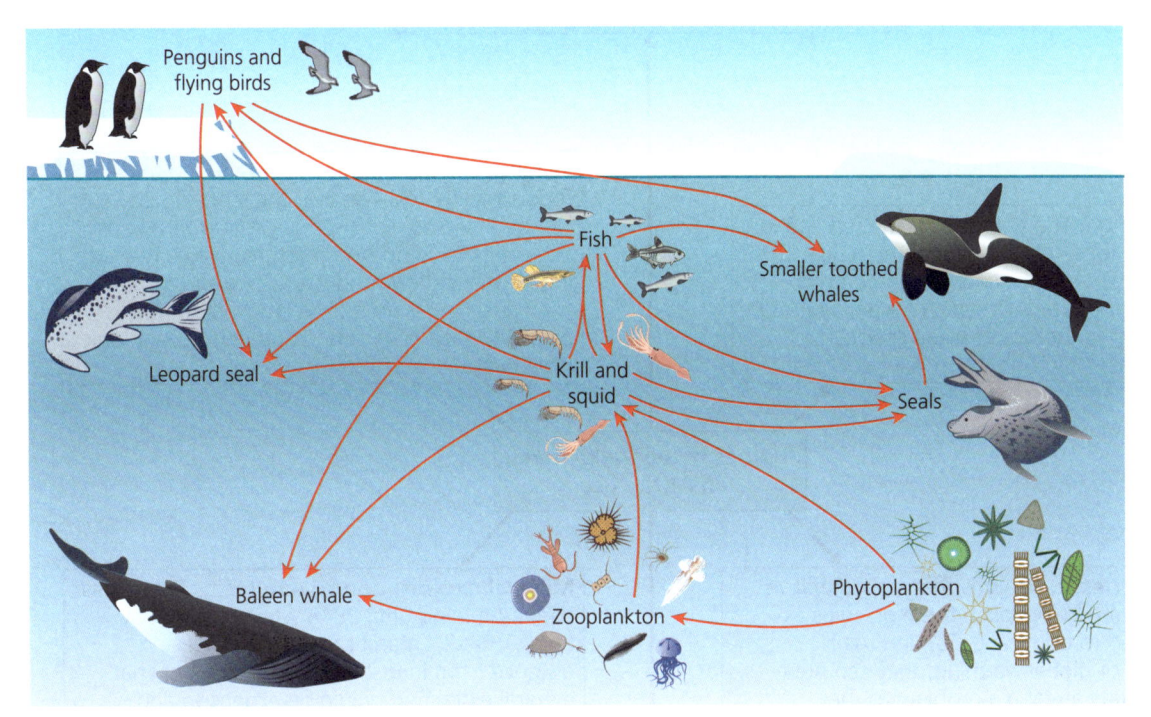

Figure 4.4 A typical Antarctic food web

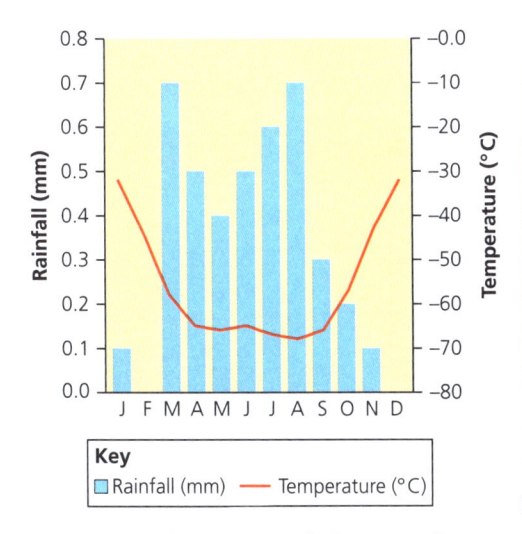

Figure 4.5 Climate graph for Vostok, Antarctica

Antarctica's future in doubt after plan for world's biggest marine reserve is blocked

A plan to turn a huge tract of pristine Antarctic ocean into the world's biggest sanctuary has been rejected, throwing the future of one of the Earth's most important ecosystems into doubt. Environmental groups said Russia, China and Norway had played a part in blocking the proposal.

The 1.8 m sq km reserve – five times the size of Germany – would have banned all fishing in a vast area of the Weddell Sea and parts of the Antarctic peninsula, safeguarding species including penguins, killer whales, leopard seals and blue whales.

'This was an historic opportunity to create the largest protected area on earth in the Antarctic: safeguarding wildlife, tackling climate change and improving the health of our global oceans,' said Frida Bengtsson of Greenpeace's Protect the Antarctic campaign.

Figure 4.6 Plans for a marine reserve

- Antarctica's tourist season lasts for just a few months in summer and bad weather can cause problems and can lead to cancelled flights.
- There is a tourist code, which asks visitors to stay at least 5m away from penguins.
- Tourists need to respect the fragile environment by following visitor guidelines under the Antarctic Treaty.
- Ships have to be 'bio-secure' and visitors are not allowed to eat, drink or go to the toilet while on shore.
- There are limits on how many people can visit at any one time, which means smaller ships are preferred, though they are more expensive.
- Greenhouse gases are emitted through the flights used to get to Antarctica and cruise ships can pollute the water.

Figure 4.7 Tourism in Antarctica

Whaling: Japan claims that it is catching whales around Antarctica for scientific purposes. In 2014, however, the International Court of Justice declared that this was just a cover for commercial hunting. Japan planned to catch 300 minke whales in 2015.

Climate change: The warming of the sea and loss of sea ice is a long-term threat to Antarctica. Already some ice shelves have collapsed and glaciers have retreated. Oceans have become more acidic, leading to the loss of some species such as marine snails.

Fishing: Any fishing boats are required to report their catches so that the stock taken can be assessed. Four species are targeted for fisheries, including Antarctic krill, which is used in pharmaceutical products. The trend for krill fishing is increasing as new markets for krill products have been found and new technologies have been used to fish for the krill.

Other human activities in Antarctica

Invasive species: Organisms that are not native to Antarctica are being taken there on ships as seeds attached to boots and clothing. As a consequence of global warming, they can now grow there. Rats are also a problem as they threaten nesting birds.

Mineral exploitation: The Antarctic Treaty has banned mining until 2048 when the policy will be reviewed. Antarctica's weather, ice and distance from industrialised areas means that mineral extraction would be expensive and dangerous. Antarctica has reserves of coal, iron ore, oil and gas.

Scientist research: There are no permanent residents in Antarctica. Scientists and support workers have lived there through multiple seasons. It costs up to $1 million a year to keep a scientist at the Antarctic, with most of the money coming in grants for research. One activity is drilling for ice cores to provide evidence of climate change. It can be stressful to be there as it is such a remote and extreme location.

Figure 4.8 Human activities in Antarctica

1 Antarctica is a polar region. State two human uses of Antarctica. *2 marks*

1 ....

2 ....

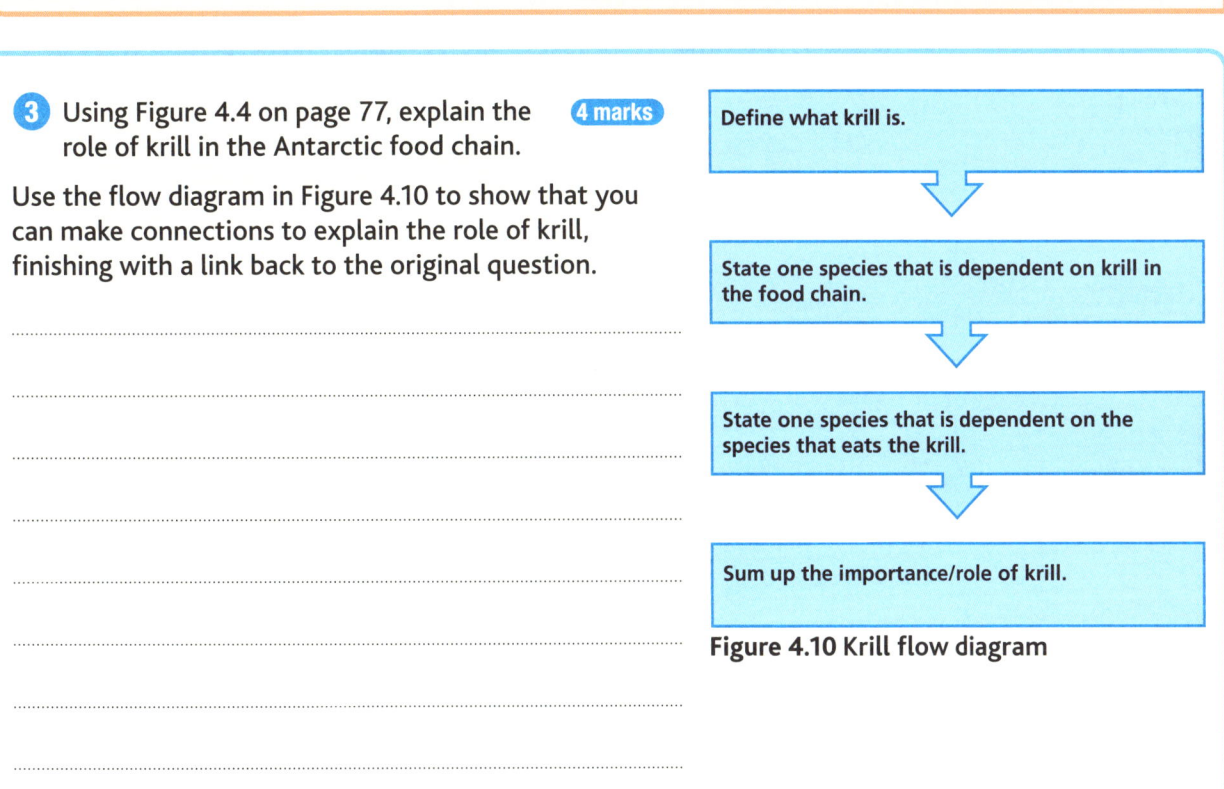

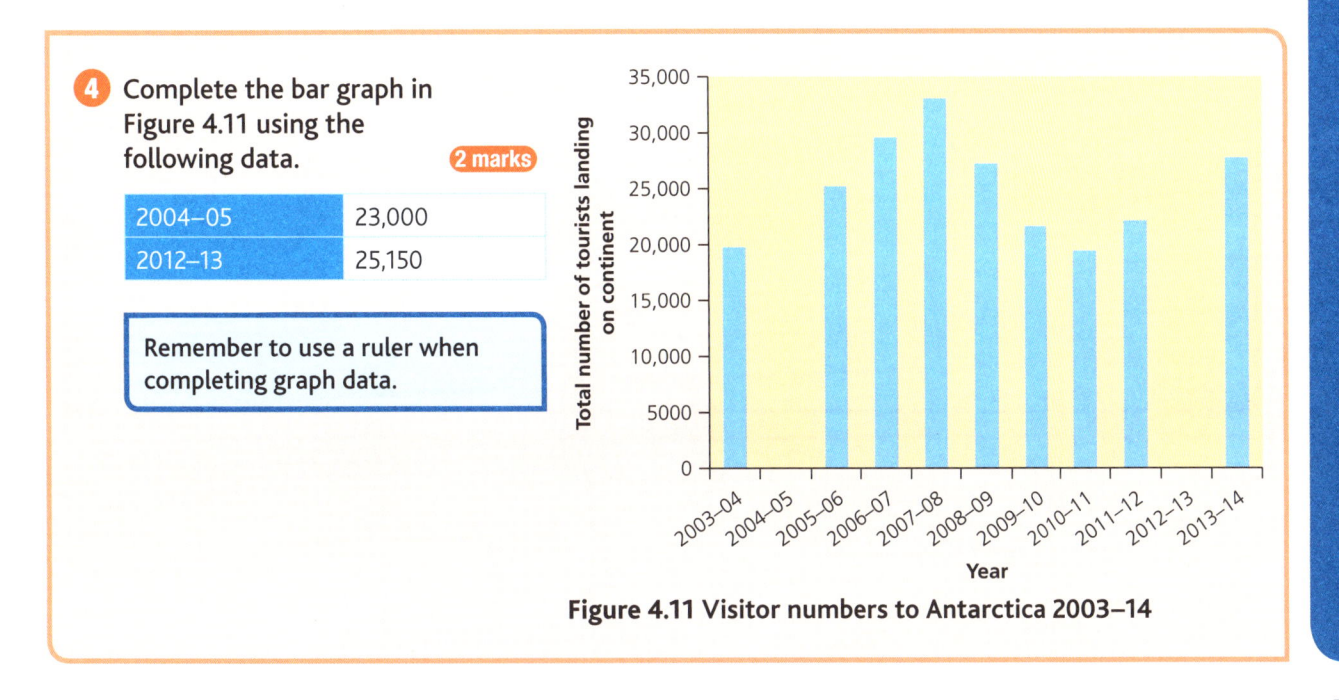

2 Using Figure 4.2 and your own understanding, describe the physical characteristics of a polar region. *3 marks*

....

....

3 Using Figure 4.4 on page 77, explain the role of krill in the Antarctic food chain. *4 marks*

Use the flow diagram in Figure 4.10 to show that you can make connections to explain the role of krill, finishing with a link back to the original question.

....

....

....

....

....

....

....

Define what krill is.

↓

State one species that is dependent on krill in the food chain.

↓

State one species that is dependent on the species that eats the krill.

↓

Sum up the importance/role of krill.

Figure 4.10 Krill flow diagram

4 Complete the bar graph in Figure 4.11 using the following data. *2 marks*

| 2004–05 | 23,000 |
| 2012–13 | 25,150 |

Remember to use a ruler when completing graph data.

Figure 4.11 Visitor numbers to Antarctica 2003–14

Chapter 4 Preparing for Paper 3

79

5 Calculate the range of visitors between 2003–04 and 2013–14. Show your workings. **2 marks**

....

....

> When answering 'calculate' questions, you often get 1 mark for the correct answer and 1 mark for showing your workings.

6 Calculate the mean number of visitors between 2003–04 and 2013–14. Show your workings. **2 marks**

....

....

7 Study Figures 4.4, 4.7, 4.8 and 4.9. For **one** threat, explain its impact on the Antarctic ecosystem. **3 marks**

Practise your use of Point – Explain – Evidence.

Point	
Explain	
Evidence	

8 Using Figures 4.2–4.5 (on pages 76–77), explain what characteristics make Antarctica distinctive.

6 marks

Mark scheme

Level 3: 5–6 marks	Level 2: 3–4 marks	Level 1: 1–2 marks
Thorough understanding of the characteristics of distinctive landscapes and **thorough** analysis of the information provided to explain which characteristics make Antarctica's landscape distinctive. This will be shown by including **well-developed** ideas about the characteristics and an analysis from the resources.	the characteristics of distinctive landscapes and **reasonable** analysis of the information provided to explain which characteristics make Antarctica's landscape distinctive. This will be shown by including **developed** ideas about the characteristics and an analysis from the resources.	**Basic** understanding of the characteristics of distinctive landscapes and **basic** analysis of the information provided to explain which characteristics make Antarctica's landscape distinctive. This will be shown by including **simple** ideas about the characteristics and an analysis from the resources.

Pay close attention to how the description of what you need to do changes from thorough to reasonable to basic understanding and analysis of the information. Well-developed ideas are also key to the success of your answer, so making connections using '… which means that …' is an essential exam skill.

There will be two 12-mark questions in Paper 3.

The first 12-mark question you encounter might give you a statement and ask you a 'To what extent do you agree …?' question, **or** it might ask you to 'explain' in greater depth. There is an example of both these question styles below and on page 83.

> It is important that you make reference to the figures in your answers.
>
> Fig … suggests that …
> According to fig …

9 'Human activity can only have a negative impact on Antarctica.' To what extent do you agree with this statement?

⏱ 15   **12 marks**

On the one hand …

On the other hand …

Overall …

How far do you agree with the statement in question 9 above? To be able to reach a clear conclusion about how far you agree with the statement, you need to write about both sides of the argument: both the **negative** *and* the **positive impacts** that human activity can have on Antarctica.

For this question, we are going to use a simple technique called 'Triple O', which stands for:

On the one hand, …

On the other hand, …

Overall, …

You can still apply your PEEL technique within each paragraph, but 'Triple O' helps you to remember to present both sides of the argument and then to reach a substantiated (supported with evidence) conclusion.

On the one hand, … **NEGATIVES**

On the other hand, … **POSITIVES**

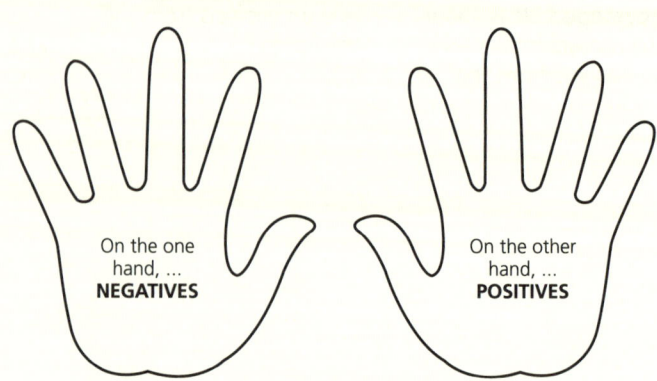

Figure 4.12 Negatives and positives

This is an example of a 12 marks question which asks you to explain in greater depth.

10 Explain how human activities affect the physical landscape and ecosystems of Antarctica.

12 marks

The examiner's advice is always to write about fewer ideas and to fully develop your points rather than writing about too many points but in an undeveloped way. In this answer, you will need to write about two or three human activities and discuss the effect they have on the landscape and the ecosystems.

11 Using the figures and your own understanding, complete your own version of the concept map in Figure 4.13 in your notebook.

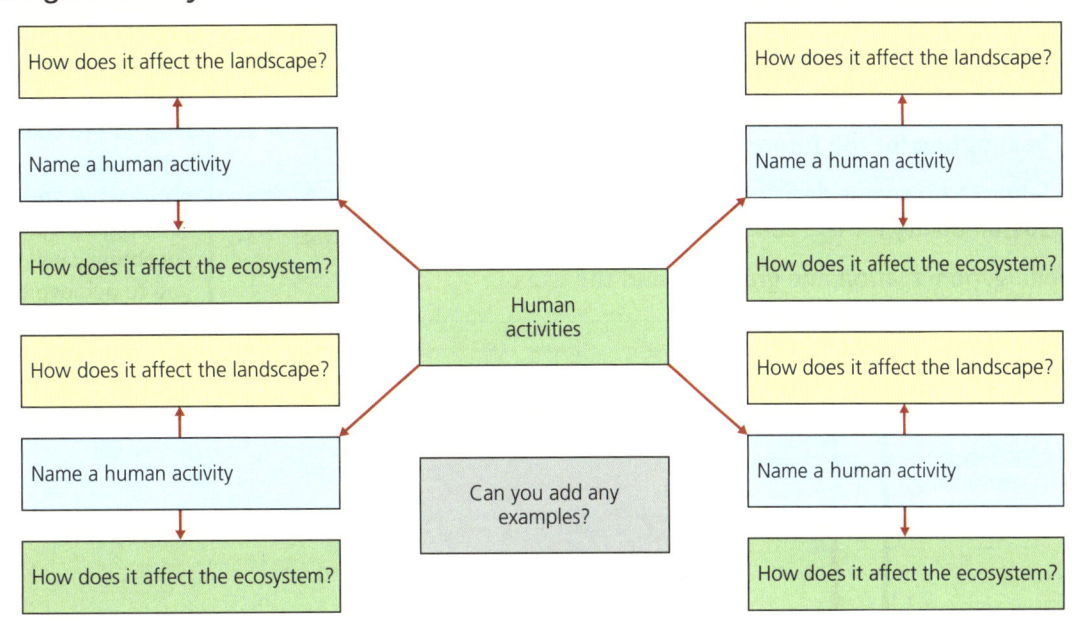

Figure 4.13 Concept map

Now that you have planned your answer, choose two or three of the human activities from your concept map to write as developed paragraphs in your answer below. (Continue your answer in your notebook if you run out of space here.)

....
....
....
....
....
....
....
....
....
....
....
....

The second 12-mark question you will have in Paper 3 is the decision-making question at the end of the paper. There will also be 3 marks for spelling, punctuation and grammar. The question will most likely be phrased one of two ways:
- You might be given two options for how a geographical issue should be managed and you choose one to justify.
- You might be asked to propose your own fully justified solution to the geographical issue.

There is an example of both of these question styles for you to practise here and on page 85.

> **12** Antarctica is facing many challenges, both physical and human, and important decisions need to be made to ensure the sustainability of the continent.
>
> 1 Examine whether you think developing more tourism opportunities or establishing a marine reserve would be the best option for the future management of Antarctica.
>
> 2 Suggest how your decision could lead to long-term sustainability for the continent. **12 marks**
>
> Spelling, punctuation and grammar and the use of specialist terminology: **3 marks**

Spend some time digesting the question. Break down the different elements of the task. Consider where you can make the synoptic links across topics. In this instance, you need to examine *both* options. Refer back to the STEEP model on page 75 to help you to consider all aspects of your chosen proposal. A good use of geographical vocabulary will allow you to achieve the highest mark.

The best option for the future management of Antarctica would be to …

This is because …

Furthermore …

One of the disadvantages of this option, however, would be …

Don't forget to make reference to the figures.

… was less likely to ensure the future management of Antarctica because …

Additionally, …

One of the advantages of this option, however, would be …

Don't forget to make reference to the figures.

This is the most sustainable decision for the long term because …

Fully justify its sustainability